Home Schooling:

Educating with Head, Heart, and Hand

Home Schooling:

Educating with Head, Heart, and Hand

J. Brian Higgins, Ph.D.

Ivy House
Publishing Group
www.ivyhousebooks.com

PUBLISHED BY IVY HOUSE PUBLISHING GROUP
5122 Bur Oak Circle, Raleigh, NC 27612
United States of America
919-782-0281
www.ivyhousebooks.com

ISBN: 1-57197-416-4
Library of Congress Control Number: 2004101268

Printed in the United States of America

To Aubrey, Vernon, Elizabeth, and Jackson.
Your devotion to each other and your generosity in sharing your lives inspire us all.

Preface

While doing research on the subject of gender issues in elementary textbooks, I interviewed an editor of a major publishing company who commented on the growing number of new orders for elementary reading textbooks that incorporated the traditional themes of patriotism, honesty, and consideration. Upon further discussion I discovered that the overwhelming majority of these orders came from the home schooled sector. I found the market viability and the focus on these particular values within this specific group of teachers/learners to be most intriguing. My formal search into the home schooling phenomenon in America thus began.

Home schooling as a viable option for education occupied a special place in my thoughts on learning ever since my daughter, Kori, entered preschool in 1993. The experience of sending my only child out into the cruel world at age five with nothing more than a Bert and Ernie lunch box and the hope that her future caretakers would live up to my expectations was truly transformative for me, as well as for the many other parents I knew. On that first day of school the emptiness that dwelt in her eyes matched the vacant spaces in that unforgettable forced smile where baby teeth used to be. Still, in the back of my mind I remembered being told that we have to learn how to socialize with others, that life isn't fair, and that out of hardship comes character. While all of these lessons of life are true, I have never been quite sure of the correct method of coming to terms with them. We do have to learn how to socialize, though learning in a cooperative, nurturing environment would certainly be more desirable than an impersonal educational institution. Life isn't fair. However, we parents and guardians do have the responsibility to ensure the highest level of fairness possible. Though character is often shaped by hardship, might it be formed better by struggle and challenge within controlled situations? Doubts and questions such as these continue to challenge my concept of the responsibilities I have as a parent and also test the philosophical underpinnings I have constructed as a teacher in the public school system.

In my public school teaching experience, spanning a period of more than 24 years in the United States and international settings, in special education and regular education classrooms, I have often found myself positioned between the competing interests of individual students and parents and those of the local school or school district. After years of personal reflection and dialogue with partners on both sides of these respective interests, I have recognized the reality that individual student agendas are most often addressed within the framework of institutional guidelines, structures, and requirements. This unwillingness to consider and employ alternatives in educational practices and procedures by public school administrators was due primarily to instances of miscommunication and misinformation, blind adherence to rules and regulations, the absence of care in schools, and, at times, unreasonable parental requests. In too many cases, sadly enough, issues of power and control by the institution overpowered the concerns parents held in advocating for the needs of their children. Ultimately, this power dynamic became the major contributing factor in the final decisions that were reached. A case in point follows.

Several years ago while I was teaching in a public middle

school, a student I knew experienced several episodes of bullying. JP was a serious student who had a true interest in learning. His peers considered him to be "uncool." Somewhat frail and small of stature, JP became a target of mistreatment. Parental concerns for his safety fell on administrative deaf ears. The principal said there was no way JP's safety could be assured as most of the bullying took place before or after school and during lunch hours. JP would just have to learn to stand up for himself. The parents offered several suggestions including the formation of a partnership with the school to monitor JP and other students more closely, but none of these suggestions satisfied the administration.

I witnessed the parents' struggle in working within principal directives with very little support from the administration. Two days after meeting with the principal, JP was in the emergency room receiving stitches in his chin as a result of a student shoving him up against a locker. The next day, JP withdrew from school and his career in home education began.

This failure by the institution to address serious problems with student behavior is just one of the many examples of the disenfranchisement that occurs frequently in our public schools. In this instance, the issue of safety had been denied. In my mind, JP was victimized on two levels: first, from the peers he encountered and second, from the educational system itself, which did nothing to support his right to attend school in a safe and secure environment.

My interest in the arena of home schooling evolved to another level upon meeting the Waterson* family during the fall of 2000. Our children were participating in a play at a local com-

*Names have been changed to protect the privacy of all individuauls concerned.

munity center. During our first meetings, the issue of home schooling entered into our conversation. We traded statistics and information about the home schooling experience with each of us revealing a passion for optimizing learning in an environment of care. At this time, I was preparing to work on a case study centered on participants and their experiences in home schooling. The Watersons seemed to be drawn to my work with great interest. I knew intuitively that they would be a wonderful participant family and agreed wholeheartedly to their inclusion. The interest on their part to be involved in this home schooling research fell in nicely with action research methodology that suggests that the participants, upon discovering meaning in their own lives in the research opportunity, invite the researcher into the relationship.

This new partnership grew from encounters such as brief conversations during carpooling situations, instructional observations, social gatherings, and spontaneous telephone conversations, to rich and insightful formal interview sessions. The research gathering process continued for more than 13 months. I will be eternally grateful to all members of this caring family for their insightful comments and devoted interest into this study.

The focus of this book is to explore the home schooling experience and how it touched the lives of this wonderful family. I can think of no better way to address this experience than through the qualitative case study method. Merriam (1998) defines the case study as, "An intensive, holistic description and analysis of a single instance, phenomenon, or social unit." Miles and Huberman (1994) frame the case study as "a phenomenon of some sort occurring in a bounded context." These researchers graphically represent a case study as a circle with a heart in the middle. This subject heart is the hub of the study, while the circle "defines the edge of the case: what will not be studied." In the case study I have undertaken, participants include a home schooled family (four members). In this study, I have attempted to capture those interactions that give meaning to the participants' experiences.

Section One: The Case Studies

This section presents the stories of four family members who share their experiences of home schooling, providing us with the opportunity to gain insight into their lives. These participants reveal to us how they give meaning to their home schooling experiences and how they interpret the value of their endeavors in the process of home education. The following interpretation of their experiences attempts to represent their words and actions faithfully through interviews, observations, and artifacts, which include student products, teacher-made materials and lesson plans. Each family member's experience has been interpreted and presented one at a time in chronological order as interview sessions unfolded over a period of 13 months. Participants made themselves available around previous commitments and activities they had scheduled.

I feel very fortunate to have been able to work with this wonderful family. I thank them wholeheartedly for sharing their experiences and insights so that we may gain a clearer understanding of home schooling practice.

Chapter One:
Aubrey's Story

Introduction

On a beautiful April afternoon, I pulled into the driveway of Aubrey's house nested in a quiet, treed neighborhood. As I walked from my car and opened the front gate, I was immediately greeted by two very large golden retrievers, tails wagging a mile a minute, tongues reaching out for any exposed patch of skin that might be available to them. These signs of affection were accompanied by whines and whistles in an air of excitement. If dogs could speak English they might have been saying, "Glad to see you again, Brian. How about scratching me right here?" Aubrey heard the commotion from the kitchen and quickly rescued me from my meeter-greeters. "Get down, you two! Go back to your places—go on." The next thing I knew, I was in the kitchen with a fresh pot of coffee staring me in the eyes and the smell of something tasty baking in the oven. At this moment, I was ready to move in with Aubrey and enjoy the cozy home environment she and her family had created.

Aubrey is in her mid-forties, about five feet, two inches tall, with light brown hair and green eyes that, according to her, turn a bluish tint in bright sunlight and red when she is angry. Aubrey is a ball of energy, probably one of the most awake people I have ever met. Her mind is constantly turning with ideas, always measuring, analyzing, and developing strategies for whatever she is doing at the moment. In the center of her life is her family. She speaks in terms of "we" rather than in terms of "I."

Throughout the house are pictures of her family, the walls replete with artwork by the kids. The refrigerator, if there is one behind the paper façade, is as much a community bulletin board as a keeper of foods, with notes concerning doctor/dentist appointments, swim meet dates, Ovation! series tickets, and anything else regarding family activities and events that lends itself to magnetization on metal surfaces. Throughout this clutter, Aubrey appears to have everything well organized and hammered down. School in this home possesses a healthy balance of seriousness and nurture, with the children occupying the central position in the whole experience.

Being at Home Again As a Woman

Our conversation began with a discussion of feminism and how the feminist movement affected her decision to home school Elizabeth and Jackson.

> *The issue of being at home again as a woman and not being in the work force earning a paycheck, that's really a huge issue, and one of the sacrifices that I consciously made*

by making this choice. I was always aware of my opportunity cost, career wise, but it [being home with her children] took priority, and so, I made that commitment.

Aubrey understood her options and made the choice to focus on the educational concerns of her children. Since first grade, Aubrey had always been involved in Jackson's and Elizabeth's educations. After searching for appropriate placements, Aubrey would volunteer in the classroom on a regular basis, assisting the teacher and her children as well as others. In her mind, choosing between the care of her children and the building of her own career was never an issue. Once she became a mother, issues of intellectual resources, educational background, and maximizing her true potential in the job market became secondary to Aubrey. Her prior experience in school and business became a resource from which she drew to provide a meaningful home schooling experience.

I used all *my education and career "wisdom" in raising my children.*

Aubrey also talked about her individual circumstances in her choice to home school and the sharing of responsibilities of home education with her husband, Vernon. It seemed that, in this case, the traditional feminine role, which included the major responsibilities in childcare, had once again been revisited with Aubrey in the home/private sphere and Vernon in the work/public sphere. These roles had been established years before for Vernon, when he was pushed and encouraged by his parents to succeed in his career field, and for Aubrey in her high school years, when she assumed many of the home responsibilities and care for younger siblings. Aubrey laments the lack of participation from Vernon in the attempt to home school their children.

If my husband had a flexible career where he could be home more, I would have definitely taken advantage of that. Ideally, that is something I would change. And it's pretty hard. At this point he is trying to take off one-half a day twice a month. Working a lot is big in his environment, and he buys into it mostly . . . Perhaps, it [home schooling] came as a choice because my husband was gone so much.

For Vernon and Aubrey, each seems to be marginalized to some degree. Societal expectations seem to have shaped the position of each parent, in Vernon's case distancing him from his family and in Aubrey's case—possibly a more complex scenario—maintaining childcare as a central expectation in her role as mother. Society gives value to those in the job market who produce a paycheck. From a certain perspective, Aubrey is in a no-win situation. She is forced to choose between two competing interests that have equal value to her.

However, in her experience, Aubrey finds that participation in the job/career field is regarded by many as the more important position and one that holds the most value in effecting a sense of internal as well as external personal identity.

Many of my contemporary women friends will not be caught back in their homes again in a financially subservient role. One struggle that I had was justifying my choice, but what's interesting is that I've had that conflict all my life because of the feminist era and because of the chauvinistic environment I grew up in. I would like to think that what has come out of feminism is that we allow for choice, and unfortunately, I feel that a lot of women aren't supporting other women's choices. Perhaps it's a threat [choosing child care for a career].

Aubrey realizes that more value is given to a woman's position if she is in the work force, which in turn commands a higher social status. In many ways, the specific job is not the determinant in this hierarchy of status, but rather the fact that a woman has a job and that she is no longer at home with her children.

You know, when my ego is suffering, I have to remind myself that I am more committed to time with my kids and also, I have to be real frank, that it's fun for me. I get sad at the fact that my kids are going to be gone in five years. So for me to take advantage of this time is a wonderful, big gift.

Aubrey goes on to say that, in spending this wonderful time at home with her children, sometimes she does feel the pull of time and effort she expends nurturing her children in opposition to utilizing that time for herself and her career. The development of her self concept is also affected by comments from friends and community members who recognize the effort it takes to home school her children, but offer no recognition or words of encouragement for this endeavor.

There is the rare person who will say, "Good for you, good choice, you're raising your children." I have many friends who compliment me on my children, but it's pretty rare to get perks from what I am doing. I mean if I told them that I was an agricultural economist they'd say, "Wow, wow, that's really neat!"

Aubrey realizes that few people appreciate the activity of home schooling.

When I tell people I'm home schooling my children they usually say, "You're crazy, you're out of your mind."

Her friends tell Aubrey that they could never home school their children. At first it really hurt her feelings, but later she learned to say, "You could do it if you chose to do it. Nobody is saying that you have to do it, but let it be a choice."

There is a certain amount of bravery that is essential to breaking the norms of behavior in choosing home school over public and private school settings. Many parents Aubrey speaks with have very real concerns about education and the low level of instruction that occurs in school. Still, Aubrey feels that it is the unusual parent who will withdraw their child from the public school classroom to engage in home schooling. Interestingly enough, Aubrey was not the one who thought of home schooling as an option; Jackson did. One day Jackson came home from school and asked Aubrey if she would home school him. It took her three years before she agreed to do it.

During the second interview with Aubrey we revisited the issue of her women friends not wanting to return to the home and possible issues related to this choice.

Aubrey commented that, from a feminist position, moving back to the home and spending all day with their kids was viewed as a definite step backwards for many women. They don't perceive it as a job choice; they perceive it as a regression. Home schooling parents don't feel that way because they think they are performing a valuable job. Their actions reflect their value system, which points to the importance of togetherness.

Aubrey revealed a direct link between parents and their children and the value to which children are assigned in our society.

> *In our society, we take our kids for granted; actually, many parents are annoyed a lot by their children. I have countless friends who just survive the summer because they have to figure out what to do with their kids. I relish the time I spend with my family.*

I could relate to what Aubrey was telling me and I proceeded to tell her a story of my own childhood when, during the summer months, my mom would take us kids to the pool, drop us off at nine sharp, and pick us up again around five. Even on rainy days with swimming gear in hand, we would pile into the old Buick, which took on a life of its own and seemed to know the most direct way to the Rosehaven swimming pool. "Have a nice day, children," she would say as we were leaving. "But mother, it's raining," I would tell her. It wasn't until years later that it occurred to me that she just wanted us out of the house.

Aubrey commented how common situations like that are and how ironic it is to think that being home with your children is viewed as a subservient role by society. In this role, the parent who stays home—usually the mother—experiences a reduction in status. This reduction in status is due to the fact that the parent at home is not connected to the production of a paycheck. Aubrey feels that in our capitalistic society, money is power and power equals decision-making rights. There are many marriages set up on that model. If a woman is home taking care of children and she is not contributing financially to the family, she loses her voice to a significant degree. This, at least, was Aubrey's experience.

> *My father earned the money, therefore he was the ultimate decision maker and ruler. There are a lot of women who have broken the mold and achieved power through the struggle of monetary might. Though women are quite capable of making decisions, often the price they pay is high.*

Aubrey's mother felt the pressure to join the work force when Aubrey was in middle school. Aubrey felt very alone during this time. Often she would come home to an empty house where she was expected to give up her extracurricular activities at school to cook meals and clean house for her parents and her four siblings. Aubrey's reaction to this was that it was unfair and sexist. Aubrey decided at the time that she would never get married and have children. She wanted no part of family life if that was the way it was supposed to be. In her later years, Aubrey reflected on this difficult time and transferred her feelings into the position of control she possesses now.

> *I reflect on those years and think, "Oh my god, my kids are going to have choices for extracurricular activities. They are not going to be lonely; somebody's going to be present when they come home from school." Also, I have a sense of security because I know what my kids are doing.*

Aubrey went on to explain that men need to be home with their children just as much as women, but because status in our society is economically driven and men usually possess a higher earning potential, women are usually the partners who assume the household and child-rearing duties.

In Aubrey's family today, she shares in the decision-making process and feels Vernon values the job she is doing at home. Aubrey is reinforced by Jackson and Elizabeth as well for the important work she does. On another level, she derives satisfaction and reward from seeing her family healthy, happy, and secure.

I asked Aubrey about her life before marriage and what effect entering into marriage in her mid-thirties had on her attitudes of family and child rearing.

Aubrey described her work experience before her marriage. Aubrey felt success in her work, but never glorified her jobs or the lifestyle that they afforded. Throughout her twenties she enjoyed being employed. She also enjoyed the freedom to travel and see the world. In her thirties, Aubrey began to want children and a family life. She questions whether or not she would have felt the struggle between career and children during her younger years.

> *I don't know how I would have struggled with that [children vs. career]. It's probably not a question of age entirely. I think I'm a person who just bonds with my children, and I'm also a one-track person. I like to do a really good job at what I'm doing.*

In a way, Aubrey dealt with the issue of competing interests of career and children by deferring marriage and child rearing to her late thirties and forties. This decision proved to be a wise choice for Aubrey, who is able to act on the values of parenting she holds. Placing herself solidly in a career track before having children and then devoting her energies to creating a nurturing family have given her positive experiences in these two important chapters of her life. In the future, Aubrey may consider a return to her former career field or retraining for a new beginning in a totally different career direction.

My Babies

For Aubrey, redirecting her focus of attention from herself and her career to her children began when Elizabeth and Jackson were born.

> *The evolution [of redirecting focus] began when they were born. They were preemies; my babies were two and a half pounds when they were born. So, before they were born I thought, "In six months, I'll be back to work." But at the time they were born, I just didn't see any alternative to overseeing their care myself.*

Aubrey went on to explain that since she and Vernon moved away from her extended family when the children were one month old, she had no one to trust with the care of her babies. Relatives now lived far away and the possibility of hiring a nanny or other outsider was not possible due to their financial situation at the time. The only way Vernon and Aubrey could have afforded to pay a childcare provider was if Aubrey returned to work.

> *It's [going back to work] a conundrum. I mean, how much would I have left over? Nothing! Under those circumstances, I don't think it would have been likely that I would have gone back to work full time. It would have been part time. Also, I wanted to be there! Furthermore, what nanny or daycare could oversee or meet the needs of two preemies?*

I have known people who were willing to go back to work,

often at minimum wage, and pay somebody else to watch their children, knowing that if they were lucky, they would break even financially. I find this perplexing though this behavior clearly demonstrates differences in the value of child rearing and the parent's participation in being employed and making money.

Aubrey commented that she felt this return to the world of work outside the home was chiefly a function of ego building. The job creates a positive identity. We asked each other, "Isn't parenting a job? Isn't parenting the most important job one can have?" We agreed that many people don't see parenting in this light and that to them making money takes priority over childcare.

In trying to come to terms with differing values of parental/child relationships, Aubrey attempts to understand her own biases and preconceived notions.

> *Perhaps I'm just too soft when it comes to my babies. The other thing is, I don't want to miss things. Once they were out of the woods medically at two or three years old . . . perhaps . . . the question is unanswerable, but I've pondered it. Maybe I was protective because they were preemies. But I had a feeling that if I had had your eight-pound, basic full-term baby that I still would have had that real deep attachment.*

To be sure, softness is no crime. Actually, if having to choose between extremes in harshness and kindness, I believe I would choose the latter. It appears that Aubrey is doing some soul searching in this section of the interview, asking herself some very hard questions. Am I overindulgent? Am I overprotective of my children due to their initial frail health at birth and throughout the first three years of their lives? Would I feel differently if my babies would have been full term and of normal weight at birth? As Aubrey states, these questions are unanswerable, though asking them gives me insight into the importance of Aubrey's feelings about the parent/child relationship.

Aubrey never thought she would home school for more than one year. In fifth grade, when Jackson asked to be home schooled, Aubrey knew that both children were way ahead of their peers in all subject areas, so she agreed to try it. What convinced Aubrey to begin home schooling was that the fifth grade class they were facing was not dynamic. There were really no teachers in the school who stood out as being able to meet Jackson and Elizabeth's needs. If Aubrey were to begin home schooling, this was the time to do it.

After Aubrey described her home schooling program, I asked her how she felt about her relationship with her children as a result of the home schooling experience. What came out of this initial question proved to be poignant and possibly one of the most important components in this study.

Aubrey thought back to the last day her children spent in fourth grade, before the children made the move to home schooling the next year. Aubrey noticed that the kids were starting to separate from her. Jackson and Elizabeth saw and heard about things classmates were allowed to do, such as staying at home alone for long periods of time and going to the mall unescorted. Jackson and Elizabeth asked why they were not allowed to do the same. Aubrey responded by saying, "We don't do that." Issues concerning rights and freedoms came up frequently. Working through these differences of opinion often left the children questioning Aubrey's intentions, which added to feelings of separation. Aubrey also noticed that the children began showing signs of embarrassment with affection.

When Aubrey and the children began home schooling, they started to read together again. Before sending her children to school Aubrey and her family read together every day, something that proved difficult during the children's formal public school education. By Christmas, Aubrey saw some dramatic changes in behavior from both children.

> *First of all, we were reading together at night. We didn't have time to do that in fourth grade. They began to want to cuddle with me. They became affectionate again. Oh my god, it was obvious. They were no longer embarrassed about loving me.*

For Aubrey, this was a major improvement. Not only did she see her children restore their love for learning, she also witnessed the return of the closeness they once had when they were younger.

Aubrey continued to talk about the gender differences she noticed between the two children in regard to the parental bond they had built with her.

Aubrey feels that Elizabeth really values the time she and her mother spend together. This mother/daughter compatibility is one reason Elizabeth wants to be home schooled now and in the future. Aubrey is flattered by Elizabeth's desire to be with her and through this positive relationship is able to structure and provide learning activities that allow Elizabeth to accelerate well beyond the normal eighth grade curriculum. Elizabeth loves to be with Aubrey, but also is able to take care of her other needs, which were mainly described as exposure to peers. At present, Elizabeth is quite satisfied with her current educational arrangement.

Jackson's is another story worth telling. Since about the middle of his seventh grade year, Jackson has been playing with the idea of returning to public school. Aubrey admits to feeling disappointed with Jackson's request. Aubrey expressed disappointment with herself as well, as if she may have not provided sufficiently for his needs.

> *Now it's not that I didn't feel some heartbreak when Jackson said, "I want to go back to school," but I have to look at the reality. I'm a mom and he's a boy, and there's a developmental thing that happens. But my hope is that if I can support him and his pursuits, maybe that will allow a closeness.*

Even though Aubrey had reservations about Jackson's return to public school, she felt the best thing for him was to follow his heart. Jackson was ready to experience the things only peer interactions can provide. According to Aubrey, Jackson had a desire to experience a social network of friends that, by the way, would include girls. At this point in his life, curiosity had gotten the better of Jackson and for the next school year, Jackson enrolled in a public charter school where he experienced success both academically and socially.

To Aubrey, home schooling accentuates the parental role. As parents, we need to allow our kids to explore new areas and at the same time, be able to set realistic limits. Balancing these two dynamics is often tricky. One of the most difficult things for Aubrey is to back off and not take hard-line approaches to her children's desire to explore and experience the world. She does her best at letting go, though she realizes that sometimes, after reflection, a firm line is best. Aubrey tries to wield this balancing act by role modeling. She exposes the kids to dilemmas she faces in her own life and discusses them with the kids. Though the kids don't always agree with Aubrey, she feels that they do respect her for the decisions she makes.

> *I notice in my struggles with Jackson, and Elizabeth too, that when they test me, if I give in, there's not that feeling of self-confidence. But if I maintain my position, there's a sense of grace that happens when they know I'm committed to doing what's best for them. Eventually, they show gratitude for my commitment.*

Aubrey chooses her battles carefully and feels that the children respect her commitment to them. The state of grace Aubrey speaks of comes about as a result of positive leadership. To Aubrey, the children perceive her actions as being in their own best interests. Though not always agreeing with her, they eventually respect her for her stand.

Schools Take Care of Things

During the interview, I had to follow up on Aubrey's feelings about other people calling her crazy for attempting to home school her children. I didn't understand why people wouldn't say, "I just couldn't do that. It's just too hard for me. I admire you for trying though."

Aubrey commented that other parents tended to rationalize inconsistencies in public education rather than critique them. These parents realized that there were problems in schools like violence, poor curriculum standards, and negative peer pressure issues, just to name a few. Aubrey commented that perhaps there may be an element of guilt at play, where parents are confronted with the home school option but instead choose to keep their kids in the public schools, despite the problems they know to exist. It could be a function of denial when parents realize the possibility for an improved learning environment for their children, but are unwilling to make the commitment in time and effort.

> *They'll say everything's fine and everything's going to be OK. The schools take care of things. We know there are very important concerns. They [parents with children in public school] just don't want to talk about home schooling.*

Certainly, home schooling is not for everyone. Home schooling does require a commitment in time, energy, and, for families with both parents working full time, finances. In my experiences with home schooling, I find that many parents cannot move beyond the first step of the consideration of home schooling as an alternative to public school.

Many of Aubrey's comments point toward a view of the public school institution as overseer and gatekeeper of knowledge that wields its own agenda in an attempt to direct the activity of schooling. This directed agenda often promotes a trained incapacity where children and parents serve the institution instead of the institution serving them. Aubrey gave an example of this by describing a neighbor's experience with a local school. This neighbor's son, who was an A student, wanted to enroll in an advanced science course, having been recommended by his science teacher. However, he would first have to pass an advanced math test. Unfortunately, the boy had some developmental delays in math. The mother searched for a tutor so her son could focus on his strengths and learn what he enjoyed. She saw her son's self-esteem fall and a loss of interest in learning. According to this parent, the school was unwilling to meet the needs of this child. The school's agenda was more important than this student's needs. In this school's attempt to take care of things, they took care to make sure their agenda was not marginalized, that their guidelines held firm, and that there were no exceptions to the rule.

Aubrey approached this same neighborhood school on several occasions and related similar stories. From a home school perspective, Aubrey wanted her kids to enroll in classes that interested them. She felt that this public school had something to offer her children. When she approached the principal with a request for part time enrollment, he flatly refused.

> *They [administrators] don't care. It's their agenda or nothing. They really don't care. They didn't say, "Hey, your kids are important, they're valuable, we're going to work with you." The reason is they want money for you. They get paid for your child if they are at least half time enrolled. The reality is, you just don't go to school and take classes. It's a matter of finding a principal who is willing to work with you.*

In Aubrey's case, the school did not take care of her. As an alternative, Aubrey went out into the community and found people who were willing to mentor her children. Aubrey also enrolled her children into organized activities such as art classes, language classes, swim teams, and other associations that supplemented their education at home. She used every resource she could find. Aubrey asked me:

> *Do you know what home schooling is? It's using the*

world to educate, and if you're an involved parent, you're doing that anyway, even if your kids are in school.

The other part of the successful home schooling equation is having children who are independent self-learners. Aubrey feels fortunate to have children who have an intrinsic love for learning with a curiosity for the world around them. Still, having children who are interested in learning accentuates the responsibility Aubrey feels in making sure her children are challenged and working to their potential. In this regard, Aubrey realizes that she needs school, especially when the children reach high school when many of the requirements in advanced classes will be beyond her expertise. Aubrey continues to research her children's educational options for the high school years ahead.

Taking That Giant Leap

Fourth grade proved difficult for Aubrey and the kids. Aubrey was a full time volunteer in Jackson and Elizabeth's classroom and put in as much time as a full time aide. Aubrey and the children perceived their fourth grade teacher as using Aubrey in activities that "glorified" the teacher. Aubrey's hard work of putting up bulletin boards, arranging field trips, printing weekly classroom newspapers, and completing everyday classroom tasks never received credit. Other parent helpers began to become jealous of Aubrey and her children, especially at report card time when her children got high marks in most areas. These other parents perceived these grades as a "favor" for the work Aubrey had done.

Aubrey was glad to see their fourth grade year come to a close and looked encouragingly to fifth grade and a new beginning. During the final days of fourth grade, Aubrey observed the next year's fifth grade classrooms and was once again confronted with mediocrity. Aubrey decided that changes had to be made and began to plan for her own home school in fifth grade. Aubrey was ready to take that giant leap. She also recognized that employees within the school sympathized with her dilemma but only offered support in ways that did not compromise the internal framework of the school.

> *Fifth grade appeared to be just a waste. It was daycare. It was a place to have them in school. There was nothing appealing about it. The principal was pretty unhappy when I left, and yet she gave me support in terms of curriculum and put me in touch with teachers who were helpful. That particular principal understood our decision [to home school] and was fairly agreeable. So I can't say that all educators were resistant and difficult.*

The children had mixed feelings about this new educational arrangement. Since Jackson had been requesting home schooling since the second grade, he was elated to begin. Elizabeth, on the other hand, said, "No way." Elizabeth was very connected and tied up in her success in school. During the summer Aubrey and the kids planned their course of study. Elizabeth was drawn into this new approach to learning and agreed to become a part of it. Elizabeth thought it would be fun and she said, "I'll try it." At the beginning of the next school year, they designed and signed a contract with timelines for work to be done.

For Aubrey, the first year was stressful. During that year, she did a lot of soul searching trying to assess her teaching abilities and making sure her children would experience success in this new school setting.

> *You know, I was so worried. I was worried about doing the right thing and doing a good job. That still stresses me out, but not as much as it used to. And one thing that I have seen is that home school kids come out successful, especially when they are working on things that they are interested in.*

During this first year of home schooling, one of Aubrey's major sources of inspiration came from David Guterson, home school advocate and author of the popular book, *Family Matters: Why Homeschooling Makes Sense.* Aubrey could relate to Guterson's experiences and found his approaches to solving problems in teaching and socialization issues very helpful. Aubrey recognizes that although she is educated, she is not educated in education. As a high school teacher himself, Guterson encourages home schooling teachers to believe in themselves. He advocates that with their child's best interest at heart and a focus on student and family interests, success in learning is sure to follow.

Aubrey also relied on the help of other home schooling families she met. She also contacted a home schooling association in the city that gave her advice. When Aubrey described her plans for her first year of home schooling, the reaction from the other home schooling families was disbelief. They commented to her, "How can you do all that in one year?" The stress Aubrey experienced during this first year was a result of the pressure she put on herself in making sure her children were successful.

> *That first year, I provided a lot of curriculum and*

structure and the other home schoolers said, "Aubrey, you're gonna die; you can't do all of this." By spring, oh my god, I was really exhausted, but we did it. Those kids probably did three grade levels in one year (laughs).

Another issue that proved difficult for Aubrey was Vernon's initial opinion about home schooling and the fact that his profession was so demanding in terms of time away from the home. Vernon did not support this home school idea, but agreed to let the kids try it for one semester only, after which they would be expected to return to either public or private school. As the year progressed and Vernon witnessed the progress the kids were making, the richness of activities, and the exposure to real learning experiences, Vernon reversed his decision and began to support Aubrey's efforts. During this first year of home schooling, though, Aubrey carried the total weight of the home schooling duties. Due to Vernon's work schedule and skepticism of the benefits of home schooling, his participation was minimal. This lack of support also added to the stress Aubrey experienced during this introductory year.

After a successful, though stressful, fifth grade year in home school, Aubrey's family once again began making plans for the middle school years. They had applied to private schools and scoped out many of the public middle schools in the area. Both Aubrey and Vernon had serious concerns about sending their children into these environments, especially considering Jackson and Elizabeth's personalities.

I felt, oh my gosh, no way. Elizabeth may be fine, but Jackson had a year in boy's choir with teasing and bullying, and I think we couldn't knowingly put him in a position like that again. I think by the end of middle school he will have skills, believe it or not, even as a home schooler.

Aubrey and Vernon were concerned with both children's social development. Jackson was kind of a loner and a very intellectual kid. Elizabeth was also unusual in a similar way, though popular and easily liked. She made friends more easily than Jackson.

I mean Jackson really brought up our anxiety, and the more I heard about [the school], the more I heard about conflicts these kids are facing. It's awful. They're getting slammed against lockers, their books and folders are getting stolen, I mean really strewn outside. Cruel and mean things are happening that they're having to deal with.

Aubrey was concerned for the safety of her children. She recognized the risks in both physical and emotional development both children would have to take as they enter into public middle school. To her family, the risk was too great. Home schooling provided a controlled environment where Aubrey and Vernon could direct learning and nurture the social and emotional development of their children, so crucial during the middle school years.

Finally, after much research, Vernon and Aubrey found a small country day school that seemed safe and supportive where they enrolled the kids for the beginning of sixth grade. At the end of the first semester and the repeated requests from Jackson and Elizabeth to return to home schooling, Aubrey and Vernon withdrew the kids and home schooled them for the remainder of the year. This second attempt at home schooling included several extended field trips and was characterized by Aubrey as more relaxed and enjoyable.

During this time, Aubrey and the kids developed their own teaching/learning rhythm and did not attempt to re-create school at home, but rather, built a community of learners concerned with each other's education, with home serving as the social/emotional base.

This format of home learning continued throughout the remainder of sixth and seventh grades. Interestingly, Jackson, who was the initial proponent for home school, was enrolled in a public charter school for eighth grade upon his request. Elizabeth, who was initially opposed to home school, would have it no other way than to continue home schooling with Aubrey. Elizabeth enjoys the independence of learning at her own pace and the ability to choose areas of study. Jackson enjoys the social aspect of his present placement, though finds the work less than challenging and the student body as a whole uninterested in learning. This current arrangement of having one child educated at home and one in public school is difficult for Aubrey, who feels pulled between these two interests, which often compromises her full attention to both children. For the time being, the arrangement will be maintained. Both children seem to be satisfied with their educational experience.

Home Schooling Associations

In support of her own home school, I wondered how Aubrey's perceptions and experiences with other home school families would affect her identity as a mother/teacher as well as her perception of home schoolers in general.

> *The longer I do it [home schooling], the more diverse I find the community really is. There is a range all the way*

from the fundamental Christians wanting to teach a Christian curriculum, to highly educated parents who want options and freedom and independence in educating their children.

In her experience, Aubrey has had exposure to the Christian home schoolers, who seem to be ubiquitous in home schooling activities. Aubrey finds that if she can be non-judgmental about their motivations and political agenda, they actually have a lot to teach her about home education because they have been doing it for such a long time.

Aubrey is involved in a home schooling group in the city. Though the group is not heavily involved in cooperative learning and teaching, they do meet once per month to exchange and compare experiences and resources. Aubrey found out about this group from a co-worker of Vernon's who was a member. This group of parents, many of whom are Catholic, tend to be highly organized and involved in interesting educational programs. Aubrey values the time she has spent with this group and feels that her home school has benefited from participation with them.

There was another group to which Aubrey had exposure for a short time, which has fallen by the wayside. They used to publish a newspaper, but as far as Aubrey can tell, this group has dissolved. This group was involved in some interesting projects and not affiliated with any religious group. According to Aubrey, there are many home schooling groups that spring up and then fade away as parents feel the struggle and commitment needed for providing education at home. Without support from all family members and the local community, home schooling can be difficult to maintain at best.

Another group Aubrey is interested in and would like to

learn more about is a home schooling group in the area that identifies itself as "unschoolers." Aubrey is drawn to this approach as she finds that self-motivated learning is the most productive. Unschooling practice embraces and reinforces the openness and trust between parent and child. It also supports and reinforces independence in learning and draws upon the natural desire each child possesses to learn and grow. Aubrey will do further research on this group in the future.

Aubrey does not like to categorize herself or her teaching style, but rather sees herself as eclectic, integrating the best components of many styles of teaching. The identification of certain styles of home education carries with it a political position. Aubrey sees many Christian home schoolers as occupying the far right; they have organized themselves to lobby for more control from the state legislature, which supports their cause. Their issues involve such things as the separation of church and state, immunization requirements, and testing initiatives that legitimize their home schooling efforts. On the opposite side of the spectrum are the home schoolers who are identified as unschooled families and others who may be termed the un-churched; they occupy the far left position and want government to stay out of home schooling practices. Aubrey places herself somewhat left of the center in this scheme of politics, though is aware of both movements and the effects that each has on her practice of home schooling.

> *It's all political. It's part of the politics of conservatism. Listen, there's a place for everybody in the world. If there are parents who want their kids tested, then test them. It shouldn't mean that you have to test your kids because I want my kids tested. You know, it's like colonizing; you shouldn't force your educational beliefs on others.*

Aubrey once again speaks of the importance of independence and her ability to shape her own curriculum as well as diminish the effects of regulations from state and federal legislative bodies.

I went on to ask Aubrey about the home schooled children she had met and if there were any characteristics they shared. I have discovered much criticism in the current literature and from direct involvement with colleagues that home schooled children are social misfits who have a hard time coping with the real world. I was interested to find out what Aubrey had to say about this.

Aubrey had a hard time trying to determine one characteristic of home schooled children. She did say, however, that one thing home schooling families have in common is that many home schooling families do not have a lot of money. She thinks this is why many home schooling families choose home education over private school. It is less expensive for one parent, usually the mother, to quit a job that may pay minimal wages at best and home school her children than to send them to private school. This is especially true with parents who have large families. Coming back to the subject of children, Aubrey did not give a characterization but rather offered observations about these individuals.

> *Home schooling children I have met are as diverse as the families they come from. You can't point them out in a crowd and say, "Hey, look at that kid; he must be a home schooler." I will tell you, as a whole, home schooling children are desirable people. They are secure; they have a sense of identity. And I'm not kidding, in most of the home schooled activities I've done, I continue to be just amazed at what wonderful kids they are. They feel loved, they have*

attention, they feel that the world is there for them to discover, and they don't hate learning.

To Aubrey, the home schooled children she has met have a positive attitude toward learning and a sense that the process of education includes the important component of self-responsibility along with a love of learning. Aubrey also commented that she felt the process of home schooling positively reinforces the parent/child bond, which is all too often absent in many family settings. It is not unusual to see a middle schooler put an arm around his/her mother or father in the social and academic settings in which she has participated. There is no substitute for time in relationship, and home schooling serves as a major facilitator in the development of close family ties.

To people who accuse home schooled children of being socially inept, Aubrey totally disagrees. Though there are individuals who have socialization problems, in her opinion, the majority of home schooled children have social skills that are completely appropriate. Aubrey does find that some home schooled children may be viewed in the "nerd" category, which probably is a reflection of their high intelligence and the fact that they are not in public school because of it. These students do not constitute the majority of home schooled children, though many people like to group all home schoolers into one category. Aubrey continues to deal with the negative public opinion associated with home schooling children.

People have a tendency to cast judgment and categorize. To be very honest with you, I had to let go of my own stereotypes when I home schooled my kids. During this process I thought, "Who says the ultimate measure of suc-

cess is to be socialized in school?" You don't have to re-create school in order to be happy.

According to her experience, Aubrey feels that home school can provide everything that public school offers and more, which does much to foster the social development of the home schooled student. Do you want to publish a yearbook? Then do so. In fact, for the last two years their home schooling group did publish a yearbook. Each family took a major part in its construction, giving the children ample opportunity for writing, photography, and editing. This wonderful experience is somewhat diluted in the public school setting where just a few students are involved with the publication of the school yearbook. Aubrey finds that because of the rich learning environment in home school, many children appear to be more mature than their public school counterparts and able to talk to adults on a higher level. Aubrey speculates that maybe this talent is viewed by some as unusual and therefore inappropriate, leading to negative stereotyping.

What Does Home Schooling Look Like?

I asked Aubrey to describe her typical day of school at home. In her experience, it seems that each day unfolded with its own nature and rhythm.

The first year, Aubrey had a schedule. The kids got up early and walked the dogs. When they returned, they would sit down and read their morning message. This message connected them to Aubrey as teacher and their learning task for the day. This morning message sometimes took the form of a newspaper article, an introduction from a nature book, or a topic of interest from the kids. Many of the vocabulary words were taken from these messages so that learning could begin at the start of each day. The educational process was generated in a large part by the kids and provided for openness and flow in the areas of study that these morning messages delivered.

> *One thing about open learning is that everything leads to something else. Everything you do will lead to a new topic. The kids can choose lizards, and one gets to read and we share that and talk about it. This is a wonderful way to connect to one another as well as to the educational process.*

Aubrey was exposed to this idea through the Quaker school that her sister's children attended. Each day, this school would begin its classes with a quiet time of reflection during which students sat quietly for forty minutes. It was magical! During this time they could raise their hands and say something they had on their minds, but for the most part it was a time for meditation. This activity seemed to center the children and allow them to consider the importance of the day ahead of them. Aubrey admits that the morning message does not always start their day in home school; sometimes math comes first due to the amount of concentration it requires. However, the morning message is seen as an important part of their home schooling experience.

Math seemed to play a central role in the children's education at home. Early in her home schooling teaching career, Aubrey joined the National Mathematics Teacher's Association for Middle Schools. She finds their monthly publication helpful with basic and enrichment math activities. Aubrey notes that Elizabeth especially took off in math due in part to the materials she received from this math association and in large part to Elizabeth's keen interest in mathematics.

Aubrey's style of teaching was very different in her first year of home schooling. She tried to create school at home. Aubrey would start the children with work at nine in the morning and would finish around three or four o'clock. Though the kids enjoyed it, Aubrey soon found herself tired at the end of each day though she realized the value and gains the children were experiencing.

> *When I first started, I would go to four and I was so exhausted. And you know what? My kids were still at it. Jackson would be asking me questions and I would just say, "Honey, give me a break! I can't do this any more; take a rest." But I will tell you, if you only home schooled three hours a day, you would be far ahead of what happens in public school.*

Aubrey began to supplement her home program with activities outside of the home that included art and language lessons, as well as swimming, which covered physical education in her children's lives. During the first year, Aubrey also provided field trips, one to the biosphere in Tucson and another to Washington, DC, where the kids served as pages for a brief period of time. Sometimes, when driving down the street, they would notice something going on and stop and discover interesting things right in their own neighborhood. One example was when they passed by a little violin shop and asked for a tour. The manager quickly agreed and took them through the process of building and repair of stringed instruments. The kids found this experience fascinating and it was the subject of study for weeks.

Writing also occupied an important part of their education at home. Aubrey required the kids to keep a "spiral." The children would record and write about their experiences on these field trips. The kids also kept a travel journal where they would often write stories of fiction, which was their favorite form of writing. Though Aubrey and her children would join the home school group and often rendezvous with the French club, most field experiences were done alone as a family.

Aubrey described her home schooling practices in a very positive light. I asked Aubrey what was the most difficult aspect of education at home and to identify any aporias, if she could. The hardest thing for Aubrey was finding a reasonable mix between facilitating a structured curriculum and offering open ended learning experiences. As time went on, Aubrey found her home school evolving from public school at home to a program of individualized learning and the construction of a teaching/learning community.

> *The hardest thing was finding balance between what you considered structured academics and open ended learning, finding a balance between your time spent at home and your time spent supplementing home instruction in community classes. There were days when I ended up trucking the kids all over town, when we didn't sit down and focus at home. So the balance, the balance is really a challenge.*

Aubrey related to me that she often felt guilty about not providing a structured lesson on days like those described above. Though, as time went on, her understanding of the educational process embraced episodes of transition and unstructured learning experiences.

Today, Aubrey comments that she feels very confident about her capabilities as a home educator. She also adds that at this point, she feels there is really nothing she can do to mess them up. She and her children can find learning experiences in almost everything they do and have proven this repeatedly throughout their home schooling time together.

In retrospect, one criticism Aubrey made of her own home school teaching was that she wasn't perfect to begin with. She admits to making many mistakes along the way. Though she did make some mistakes in experimenting with teaching techniques and proficiency levels of subject matter, just like any first year teacher, she felt a strong sense of responsibility for her position of teacher/parent. During that first year, Elizabeth and Jackson started a math program at the same level, but as time went by, Aubrey realized that the children had to proceed at their own pace. Elizabeth wanted to take off, where Jackson became somewhat rebellious about completing his assignments. Seeing Elizabeth leaving Jackson behind in math was hard for Aubrey. She realized that for a while, she had been holding Elizabeth back for Jackson's sake. She was worried that he would fall by the wayside and in turn, jeopardize his self-concept. This event also made Aubrey question her abilities as a teacher. For a while, she felt that she had failed Jackson, but eventually she determined that each child must learn at his/her own level and rate. Aubrey had the realization that to a large degree, public schools operate on this principle of grouping multi-level students together, which holds some students back, frustrates others, and focuses on the small group of students in the middle. Self-esteem certainly is an important issue in education. Aubrey realizes the reality that her children are different, with their own strengths and weaknesses. Each child must be able to discriminate between his or her abilities and perceptions of value as human beings.

It's Not Elitism, It's Independence

Throughout this research on home schooling, I have found that the most frequent concern with this educational activity is that of elitism. People from all walks of life would ask me, "Why do you want to study this educational option that encourages elitist principles while at the same time supports right wing Christian fundamentalists?"

Aubrey addressed this issue by talking about her observation of other home schooled families and, of course, by discussing her own experiences. Aubrey realizes her opinions and family situation might not be representative of other home schooling families.

> *I have this little conscience that says maybe I should caveat this by saying I am probably not representative, but I don't find the home school community elitist at all. The people [home schooling parents] I like most and have the best relationship with are very tolerant with what goes on in school; in fact, many of them have older kids in school part time. It's independence, not elitism; it's independence that you achieve. There's a very big difference.*

Aubrey illustrates her point through an experience at a public school as she attempted to enroll Jackson and Elizabeth in seventh grade.

Aubrey approached the school with a plan for part time enrollment but found that the principal was too demanding in terms of his own agenda. Aubrey wanted to choose specific classes for her children but was told by the administration that this was not possible. Aubrey felt that there were many things from which her children could benefit, and that since she is a taxpayer, she should have access to the services public schools offer. The principal refused to consider any accommodation and the conversation was over. According to Aubrey, the public agenda is just not set up for modification. The sentiment is that you are causing us too much work, and we would be doing you a favor by enrolling your children part time and allowing them to select classes they request.

This situation is not indicative of elitism, but rather a story about the lack of flexibility in public schools and its desire to ignore the needs of students. Why couldn't the principal accommodate a part time schedule? Issues of power, control, and finances will be discussed later in this regard.

Aubrey commented that she didn't think herself better than the teachers or administrators who operated the school. In fact, she felt that she had much to learn from them. She would love to share a partnership with them but has yet to find a situation where her voice is valued or where her sense of independence can be facilitated.

> *I don't think I'm better than all the educators. In fact, my insecurities and stress come from this feeling that the educators may know things that I don't know. I'm learning as a first year teacher would learn, but I've also been learning since they [my children] were born. I know more about my kids as individuals than the educators, and that's where I have the advantage over them.*

To Aubrey, the feeling of independence is incredibly exciting. Her first attempts at home schooling were characterized as a re-creation of the public school classroom at home. In the evolution of their home school, Aubrey found more and more opportunities for learning outside the normal classroom settings and activities. The most success was discovered when she was able to reformulate her ideas about the nature of education instead of trying to structure it like the classroom and schools. Aubrey admits that sometimes you do have to sit down at a desk and complete those math problems or vocabulary lists; there's no way around it. However, there is no substitute for capturing those learning moments that present themselves in the everyday experiences to which we are exposed.

> *It's the independence. We can sit down and read the world news and at the end of the week have a discussion. With the kids in school full time, that probably wouldn't be happening. The kids can visit Vernon at work any time. My kids probably have more career education than I ever had, because if we find somebody in a career field, we ask them, "Hey, can we visit you at work?" You know, there are opportunities galore.*

Framing the practice of home education in a context of independence rather than elitism provides insight into Aubrey's positive perspective of home schooling. I asked Aubrey to talk about the perception people may have that the reason she can home school is because she and her husband are both professionals and can afford to do so. What about individuals and families who can't engage in home schooling activities due to the loss of income of one parent staying home? And, finally, I asked Aubrey if she thought it was fair that she and her family can home school while others can't.

> *I don't buy that. When I had my babies, I had people saying to me, "Well, you can stay home because your husband's a doctor." And I said, "Would you like to know how much he's earning in his training?" We qualified for WIC.*

We were on welfare when my babies were born because we all of a sudden became a family of four. It's an irrelevant argument. I don't buy it. It shortchanges you. I made the choice. When my babies were born, they came first. I just couldn't compromise their welfare knowingly.

Aubrey's choice was to stay home with her babies. To her, the level of family income was a decision that was made by Vernon and herself. Aubrey spoke about the importance of a social conscience and the consideration for those who are in need of aid. Making considerations for others who may not be as fortunate and meeting the needs of your own family are not mutually exclusive. To prevent Aubrey's family from home schooling because others do not is simply not fair.

Throughout this portion of our conversation, both Aubrey and I were troubled by the word "elitism." I asked her to interpret the word for me so I might have a clearer understanding of how she was using it. I asked her what people mean when they say home schooling is elitist.

I guess I feel that it means that you are making a special exception for yourself and you're implying that you're deserving of something that everyone else is not. If you want to look at the American way, the opportunity for individual choice is on the list. Besides, I wasn't chosen; I chose it.

Aubrey made a wonderfully insightful distinction between being chosen and making an individual choice. When speaking of elitism in schools, I would like to ask the reader what she/he thinks about a group of students in public school who are excused from classes, who ride in special buses, and wear special clothes reserved for them only, and whose association and membership in a certain club provides a higher social status than other students. On top of this, handicapped students and females need not apply. Of course, what I am referring to is the typical high school football team where members are chosen by a select group of individuals known as coaches, who reinforce all of the above conditions. From this example, we might refine our definition of elitism to include the component of being chosen for participation in a group that screens individuals for membership. In home schooling, participants are not chosen, but rather choose their educational option. Using this definition, many private schools could be termed elitist when considering the academic requirements that must be met before membership is offered. If we are offended by the perceived elitism in the home school situation, certainly the blatant display of elitism in other forms of mainstream educational options, as well as certain associations offered within our public schools, should come under criticism as well.

The Epiphany: Education Often Has Little to Do with School

> *You know, what has happened since Vernon and I have begun home schooling our kids is that we discovered this whole other side of education that has nothing to do with school. The biggest lessons I have learned in my life have nothing to do with school.*

Aubrey goes on to talk about one myth of schooling that states that if you educate yourself, you will become successful. During college, Aubrey began meeting people from all walks of life and found out how they made a living. Some of the most successful people she met were entrepreneurs who probably had eighth grade educations at best. In defining success, Aubrey believes education offers a certain quality of life though it doesn't necessarily correlate with income or time spent with family.

> *That [income and spending time with family] is based on ingenuity. There's a certain talent in finding jobs and making jobs for yourself. . . you don't learn those things in school. You learn history dates and how to do math. Schools do not correlate education with real-world decision-making. That is becoming clear to me.*

I asked Aubrey how the home schooling experience addresses issues of making the connection between life's activities and success.

Aubrey's honest answer to this question was, "I don't know." Aubrey believes that some teachers do make meaningful attempts to connect learning to life, but—in criticism of public education in general—these attempts often fall short of meeting student needs. Providing children with a holistic picture of the world and providing them with support in finding a job at the end of their educational experience in high school and college would certainly ease the inevitable process of finding one's way in the world.

Critique of Public Schools

Central to the decision to home school her children was the critique of public schools themselves. Aubrey gave much thought to the structure of public schools, the influences present in the schools that discouraged her, and things that were missing in the public schools that would definitely make them better.

Aubrey's first comment focused on teachers. First and foremost, she recognized the importance of the job of teaching and the almost impossible position in which teachers are placed every day. These people are responsible in a large part for preparing our children for the future and this hugely important job should be given more status. Aubrey also recognized that teachers in her state are underpaid and overworked. She felt that the result of these conditions played themselves out in low self-esteem, poor motivation, and the lack of a willingness to work in the best interests of children. In short, Aubrey experienced many teachers in the local school system who were burned out. She felt that the worst part of all was that the majority of teachers were unhappy in their jobs. In further reflection on teachers and the difficult job they have, she felt that any classroom was just as good as the students in it and the degree of cooperation they display.

> *The problems we have in schools aren't really the school's responsibility, and I don't know if they can solve them. They're trying; they're trying desperately. I think a lot of the problems that exist are family problems. What we have is a whole population of lackadaisical parents who don't care about consequences. That leads to an environment where education isn't even the priority. Furthermore, the school's hands are being tied to a large extent.*

I was intrigued by Aubrey's comment on schools and followed up with the question that if education was not the priority of schools, what was?

Aubrey wanted to make it clear that she felt schools did value education, but that students were not coming to school with an attitude reflecting the value for learning. From her experiences, Aubrey felt that the priority of schools today is behavior management. There are so many children in school who require inordinate amounts of time from the classroom teachers in order for them to behave in the most basic ways. To Aubrey, it gets even worse in middle school.

> *Probably one of the hardest things for us [Vernon and Aubrey] and for my kids was dealing with behavior kids. It really isn't fair that you're waiting half of your classroom time for other kids to settle down. And the teachers, as far as I can tell, are not really trained in general to deal with that stuff. I'm not sure I'm trained. I don't really fault the schools. It's the situation. It's unsolvable in this specific period of time I have to educate my kids.*

One of the major determinants in Aubrey and Vernon's decision to home school was the concern over the issue of violence in public schools. Aubrey had read enough articles about guns in schools, both nationally and locally. She had read about the presence of guns in America's elementary schools, and though there have been no reports about elementary schools in her city, she feels they are there and that it's only a matter of time until their presence is felt.

Aubrey was also concerned about assault in schools. She knew several kids who had been seriously threatened in school. When voicing her concern to other parents, many told her that her kids would have to learn how to deal with threatening situations just like their kids were. Aubrey felt differently about this issue. She feels that she has control over their environment and that it is her responsibility to shape this environment as much as possible to exclude serious risks that may do harm to her children. She knows bullies are out there, and she feels that her kids are not yet ready to deal with overly aggressive people.

Aubrey perceives that Elizabeth is better able to handle herself in situations of bullying. Elizabeth is pretty sure of herself in terms of physical boundaries due to attention to issues of physicality that Aubrey discussed with her throughout her school years. Of course, Aubrey realizes that Elizabeth could be victimized. It is our job as parents to teach our kids what to do and how to deal with issues of violence and aggression. Sometimes that includes avoiding dangerous and unnecessary situations.

Another serious concern Aubrey voiced was centered on the school curriculum. Having spent many hours in her children's public school classroom as a parent volunteer, Aubrey recognized that what's going on was very basic instruction. Much of what goes on in the classroom is "behavior stuff." Aubrey has read and heard about wonderfully creative and progressive educational programs and wants her children to be in them; however, she has had a hard time locating them. There have been numerous articles in popular magazines such as *Time* and *Newsweek* that showcase innovative schools, many of which, strangely enough, are in inner-city locations. She realizes some of it is media hype; however, reading about these excellent schools certainly plants the seed for possibilities in Jackson and Elizabeth's own educational future. Aubrey and Vernon continue to search for that special public or private school that will encourage and facilitate a learning partnership among all stakeholders.

Bringing Home into the School

After listening to several hours of tape-recorded conversations with Aubrey, a synthesis of her ideas evolved into the idea of bringing home into the schools in an effort to support teachers and make the educational process more generative and meaningful to students and their families. One example of bringing home into the school is a grandparents' program I had been exposed to while supervising student teachers in a rural elementary school. These seniors became part of the classroom community. Their presence added a calmness and caring that I seldom experienced in other classroom settings. I felt this program contributed to the quality of providing a sense of home in the school.

Aubrey gave examples of her efforts to bring a sense of family into the classroom. When Jackson and Elizabeth were in first grade, she would go to school with them and read stories to the children. Aubrey would take small groups of children and try to get to know them. Without her assistance or the help of other parent volunteers, it was almost impossible for children in this first grade classroom to connect with an adult during school. Parent participation in the classroom would be a wonderful first step in bringing home into the school.

> *I remember reading to the little kids in first grade. I loved those kids! I always got attached to them and was amazed at their level of neediness compared to their level of ability. Since classrooms are so big and schools can't hire people to help in the classrooms, parents need to be there.*

Aubrey noticed the relationship between student ability and need for supervision in educational experiences throughout the day. There were some children who had never been read to. Many of those children required additional assistance in behavior management and, of course, early academic training. Aubrey suggests that reading remediation efforts should include the parent who can extend the remedial efforts of school. In addition, real attempts to include the student and his/her family and cultural background into the educational equation would be a great motivator in the learning process.

> *Somehow, you have to figure out how to get them [parents] in. They need to show their culture. They need to feel like they're important. They need to be able to share their story, their culture to their kids. There has to be a way to include them so that they can see the beauty in it. One of the most beautiful things is reading to your children . . . It's so true.*

Aubrey recognized that some students who require individualized attention from the teacher are often from households where the parents do not reinforce the school program. Getting these parents into their child's classroom is a difficult task, possibly due to their lack of interest in the educational process to begin with and also because many children come from homes where both parents work. It is almost impossible for many parents to come to school during their work hours. It will require innovation to bring parents into the schools. Aubrey is optimistic about this partnership, though she realizes that first there must be a genuine desire on the school's part to regard parents as valuable members in their community.

Home Schooling in the Future

One of the last things Aubrey and I talked about concerned the part home schooling will play in her and her family's life in the future, and how she sees the home schooling movement progressing in the years to come.

The first thing that came to Aubrey's mind was, "to home school or not to home school." Today, she doesn't see many educated women choosing to stay home with their children. In fact, Aubrey sees most women moving in the other direction. Aubrey recognizes a trend for women to hold on to their jobs and careers though she has read about a new progressive movement in the United States where well-educated mommies are choosing to stay home with their babies. Women involved in this movement view this move back to the home as liberating and consider the time at home to be in society's best interest. Aubrey hopes people will consider home schooling as a viable option for families who search for educational options. To Aubrey, it doesn't have to be a reaction to poor learning situations in public and private schools, but rather a first choice for many families who value and would like to achieve that ideal family unit.

To Aubrey, David Guterson's book, *Family Matters,* describes the perfect family where individual learning is achieved through working together. Working together as a family does not imply conformity, however. It is more the case that each child is encouraged to find his/her special interests and talents in the environment of nurture and encouragement from all family members. Aubrey encourages anyone who is interested in exploring the subject of home schooling or building a cohesive and loving family to read this inspirational book.

The future for the home schooling movement is uncertain in Aubrey's mind, and in a way this uncertainty is frustrating. All her experiences tell her that home schooling provides a wonderful form of alternative education to public and private school. For Aubrey and her family, her direct involvement in home schooling depends on the needs and desires of her children. As stated previously, Jackson is presently enrolled in a public charter school where he is experiencing a good degree of success. Elizabeth is still being home schooled and is also very happy in her present educational environment. Though home schooling in high school is somewhat more difficult than in the earlier grades due to graduation requirements and the units of credit that must be achieved and documented, there are ways of fulfilling these requirements at home. Aubrey has researched the different associations and educational companies that provide, for a cost of course, approved curriculum and courses of study for grades nine through twelve, whereupon completion the student receives a high school diploma. Also, many home schoolers, after their sixteenth birthdays are free to take the GED. Upon successful completion, they receive the equivalent of a high school diploma allowing them to apply for jobs that require a diploma and make application to colleges and universities to further their educational careers.

One trend Aubrey recognizes is that more and more colleges in America are adapting their entrance requirements to accommodate home schooled students. Due to their success record in institutions of higher learning, home schoolers are being embraced by many colleges and universities that recognize the advanced levels of thought and academic achievement they bring with them.

At present, Aubrey and Vernon are searching for public

and private high schools that may meet the needs of their children. Aubrey and Vernon are also considering home schooling during Jackson and Elizabeth's high school years. Their decision will depend on the public and private school programs available to them and the children's desire to enter into home education or the other options made available to them during their ninth grade year.

Chapter Two:
Elizabeth's Story

Introduction

It was late spring in the high desert. The winds had embarked on their annual ritual of racing through the town and pushing the branches of mighty trees in any direction they chose. Leaves and debris were flying through the air putting on a show for Elizabeth and me as we began our early afternoon conversation in her home about her experiences with home schooling.

Elizabeth had just turned thirteen at the time of our interview and was wonderfully receptive to my request to talk with her. If anybody could be described as cute, it would be Elizabeth. With medium length brown hair, sparkling brown eyes, and a smile that says, "I think I know something that you don't," she seemed to be always up to something. Elizabeth can be described as a warm person with a kind and generous heart. Throughout the interviews I found her to be a reflective girl, preferring to tell me nothing, rather than offering an incorrect or misleading comment. Elizabeth has a highly developed sense of humor and I have noticed that everyone enjoys being in her company. For me at least, I couldn't think of a more wonderful way to spend this beautiful afternoon.

My First Memories of School

Elizabeth's memories of school were positive from the very first day. Elizabeth did well in school and hated to miss anything that may have gone on in her absence.

> *I think I liked school, and I didn't ever want to miss a day. Even when I was sick, I wanted to go. When I was in first grade, I got sick in school and I begged my mom not to let me go home. I don't know, I just liked school. I didn't want to miss anything.*

Elizabeth's love for school and learning began at a very young age. Elizabeth found success during her early school years due to her academic abilities and the fact that her parents spent countless hours with her and her brother reading together and learning as a family. Elizabeth never really felt the anxiety of parental separation to the degree that some children experienced, in part because her mother was a frequent visitor to the classroom where she interacted with Elizabeth as well as the other students in class. In a way, Elizabeth had come to school bringing her home and family with her.

Only part of Elizabeth's success was due to the teachers she had during these early years of public school. There was one teacher that she really loved, though she had others she described as just OK. To Elizabeth, the difference between a good teacher and a not so good teacher is clear.

What's a nice teacher? Well, they don't scream a lot. My third grade teacher was great. She did all these things like projects. She did days where you had to dress up. Then she had these tables where you had to wear thinking cap. We wrote books and drew pictures. It was pretty neat!

It is fairly clear that Elizabeth experiences success and joy in learning in an active environment where she is able to interact with others in project-oriented, thematic-based curriculum.

Elizabeth described her third grade teacher as nice. To Elizabeth, a nice teacher gives the students rewards for doing a good job or for proper behavior in the classroom. A nice teacher also does not yell at the kids, but rather treats them with respect. Using Elizabeth's third grade teacher as an example of a good teacher shows that a good teacher also teaches. Elizabeth felt that she learned a lot during her third grade year. This teacher combined an active classroom setting with a variety of learning experiences that included computers. Elizabeth really liked working with technology in the classroom.

Elizabeth remembers another teacher that she also liked, though she detected a definite teacher preference for girls. Elizabeth was one of the star students in this classroom. This teacher also did many interesting projects. Throughout all the interesting classroom experiences, Elizabeth was cognizant of this teacher's unfair treatment of the boys. Elizabeth had a hard time understanding why the teacher did not like certain boys who she, herself, regarded as good, hard-working, polite students. According to Elizabeth, this teacher would praise the girls and ignore the boys in class. When the teacher left the room, she always put the girls in charge. If the boys talked in her absence, the girls would put the boys' names on the board, which would get them in trouble. Though Elizabeth was never the object of unfair treatment from the teacher, many of her friends were. The potential for unfair treatment of certain students was one reason why the family considered home schooling.

The Perfect Teacher!

During the interview, Elizabeth often made mention of the perfect teacher. I asked Elizabeth to describe the perfect teacher to me.

To Elizabeth, the perfect teacher lets the kids do what they want to do. She is not talking about a classroom without rules, but rather an environment that is structured around the academic strengths of each child. In Elizabeth's case, this would be math. Elizabeth would love to spend at least half the day working with math. Other kids who enjoy writing and spelling would be doing that. Elizabeth feels that teachers should give little treats when kids do a good job on their work. She admits that this approach is somewhat "kindergartenish," but for some kids it might help them get their work done.

The perfect teacher also needs to be able to keep the kids in line. The teacher must be strict to a point but be kind to her students also. For Elizabeth, she does best in a classroom where the teacher has definite rules and a daily schedule where she knows what is expected of her. Direction from the teacher in a structured environment is very important for Elizabeth. In describing the perfect teacher, Elizabeth commented that her mom was a great example of what the perfect teacher should be. Elizabeth's mom pushes her and challenges her in a kind and gentle way. Some people may see it as sort of mean but Elizabeth trusts her mom and knows that she wants the best for her. In home school, Elizabeth often gets enrichment activities that really make her stretch and think about what she is learning. Elizabeth loves a challenge.

Elizabeth's concept of the perfect teacher has more to do with learning than individual personality. Elizabeth feels that as long as she learns, she can be happy with about any teacher she has. Elizabeth mentioned several teachers who were "hateful," but she has the ability to look past this personality flaw and direct her attention to evaluating her own progress on the learning curve. On the other hand, Elizabeth spoke about a teacher who tried to be very nice but was not the best teacher in the world. This teacher would say, "Go do this" but would not really tell the kids how to do what she was asking. Also, Elizabeth commented that this teacher was not organized, "And you know, to be a good teacher, you have to be organized!" Another characteristic this teacher possessed was that of "taking over." Elizabeth viewed this as a way of the teacher having power over her students and sometimes over the parents who would volunteer in the classroom. This did not make for the best classroom. Elizabeth also had to rely on her mother to give instruction on assignment completion and comprehension throughout the year with this teacher. Elizabeth felt that in this setting she learned basically nothing with this teacher. In many ways, it was a waste of time.

In a perfect world, Elizabeth would choose a teacher who possesses a caring personality and who structures her classroom in a challenging and enriching way. Elizabeth has seldom experienced the perfect teacher with anyone else other than her mother. To Elizabeth, her mom does a wonderful job of teaching her the things she needs to know in a way that makes learning interesting. This is quite a compliment for Aubrey, who would probably get a superior rating from her most critical evaluator.

The Beginning of Home Schooling

Elizabeth did not like home schooling at first. When her mom mentioned the idea, Elizabeth immediately objected.

> *I didn't want to home school. I wanted to be with all the kids. I wanted to be in the classroom. I liked the teachers and I liked the principal.*

Things in school were going fine for Elizabeth. She experienced success in her studies and formed a social network that she enjoyed. Elizabeth agreed to home school after constant exposure to her mother's planning initiatives for the following year. Once Elizabeth began the year at home, she immediately discovered the accelerated pace she could set for herself and the really interesting ways of approaching schoolwork.

> *In fifth grade, I really liked it when I started to progress, and you know, Mom did all these cool field trips. I also started doing all these other activities too. I do science class, art class, French class, and swimming. That's where I get most of my social contact.*

All of the classes with the exception of swimming are composed mostly of other home schoolers. The social component of education and schooling was a subject of concern for Elizabeth. Elizabeth enjoyed the time she spent with her peers in school.

At first, Elizabeth had some reservations about the typical

home schooled kid, though after meeting home schoolers her impressions changed.

She does characterize some home schoolers as "definitely awkward," but also realizes that these somewhat awkward kids are everywhere. Elizabeth spoke of one friend who is home schooled, but who doesn't come to any of the activities she once attended. According to Elizabeth, this girl's mother will not allow her to interact with other children anymore. This girl is now in a home school group mostly comprised of younger children. Elizabeth worries about this friend and feels that this friend's present situation may not be a good one. Elizabeth also talked about three kids she met in French class who were really neat and fun to be with. They interacted wonderfully with the other kids and the teacher as well. Elizabeth concluded that it really doesn't matter if you are in home school, public school, or private school. A person's behavior and social skills really depend on his/her personality.

Elizabeth's first steps into the world of home schooling were accompanied with uncertainties about the lack of social exposure to other kids and the new identity and self concept that would evolve as a result of her move back to the home. Consistent with her personality and learning traits, Elizabeth seemed more concerned with this social aspect of home schooling than with the academic experience she would have. Because Elizabeth is a serious student, she knows she is able to learn in just about any environment. It is interesting to note that in my experience of talking with home schoolers, Elizabeth's concerns are shared by many children and adults in their move to home schooling. Issues of social contact and society's perception of home schoolers are often a major concern for families who consider this educational option.

Home Schooling? What the Heck Is That?

Elizabeth's home schooling involvement was born from her brother's desire to try this option for education. Since the second grade, Jackson, Elizabeth's brother, made several requests to home school because of the many friends he had that were home schooling. At first Elizabeth had no idea what home schooling was. When it was explained to her and she understood that she would no longer be going to school, she wanted no part of it.

> *Home schooling? What the heck is that? I didn't want to go. I didn't want home school, but when my mom said we'd go on field trips, we're doing this and that, I said, "I'll try it out for one year." After the first week, I really liked it.*

Though it did take some convincing at first, Elizabeth grew to love the home schooling experience and today would have it no other way. Elizabeth and Jackson went to a private day school after the first year of home schooling because, according to Elizabeth, her mom was totally burned out. Their first year of home schooling was intensive. Though both Elizabeth and her brother made fantastic gains in their work, Aubrey felt the stress of organizing and implementing a meaningful home school program. After one semester in this private day school, upon the request of both Elizabeth and Jackson, they once again returned to the home for school. Today, Elizabeth continues to home school while her brother attends a public charter school. Elizabeth is delighted to be in her present educational setting.

I asked Elizabeth to describe her typical day in home

school during seventh grade. Elizabeth immediately talked about the trips she had taken and how wonderful they were. Extended trips were somewhat dependent on whether Elizabeth's dad could get off work or not. When he could, they would take trips that would sometimes last for a week. Mostly their trips were short, lasting for a period of half a day to an entire day or two. Elizabeth spoke of the "spiral" she and her brother would keep. Her spiral is a notebook in which she records all of the experiences and impressions about what she has seen. This spiral serves as a journal as well as a vehicle for narrative, fiction, and non-fiction writing. This spiral, which consists of at least two hundred pages, contains opera tickets, photographs, announcements, and writings of all the important things Elizabeth has experienced while on her trips. I would describe this spiral as a scrapbook on steroids just waiting for another deposit of lived experiences. Elizabeth was kind enough to share it with me, and I have spent countless hours looking through it in wonder.

What impressed me most about the spiral was Elizabeth's attention to detail in her writings about the events she experienced. The entry on *Phantom of the Opera* was written with wonderful descriptions on black paper with white ink. This writing and the way she presented it captured the mood of the whole play. Farther back in the spiral, Elizabeth wrote about the exhibit she attended at a local museum. According to her artifacts and writings, this was a comprehensive showing of the world of the Middle East, which included their conquests, arts, history, form of government, and geography. Elizabeth's writing revealed to me the high level of understanding she possessed in connection with this exhibit. It was also obvious that Elizabeth conducted research and other follow-up activities in connection with the exhibit and incorporated her work into her home school studies. After telling me about the trips, Elizabeth went on to discuss the average day of home school.

Elizabeth stated that school is different each day of the week but that in general their day in home school usually begins at nine o'clock. Elizabeth is a self-starter and she begins her studies without her mom having to tell her. Elizabeth works in her own room, as does her brother. Her mom gives her a test almost every day and Elizabeth grades it herself. When Elizabeth needs help, she asks and her mom is always there for her. Elizabeth tries to finish her math lessons first thing because she concentrates best earlier in the day. After math, she would occasionally ride in the car to Jackson's piano lesson. In the car while waiting for Jackson, she might work on geography or writing since those two subjects were integrated. Elizabeth especially liked the writing she did connected with her geography studies.

After lunch, Elizabeth would usually work on a project of her choice. Projects and research areas on which Elizabeth would work were totally up to her. Though her mother would sometimes help her get started, Elizabeth had complete control over the subject of her study.

> *OK, if I am interested in something, let's say I'm interested in Greece, I'm gonna learn everything I can about Greece. I can make a flag. I can make a costume. Basically, you could do a report on anything you want!*

I asked Elizabeth if she could do a research project on warthogs and she said, "Sure, I could do it on anything I want. Warthogs are animals. You could figure out where they came from, like what species." Elizabeth seemed excited about letting me know she had control over her learning and that she played a large part in her educational programming.

Next in the day, around four o'clock, Elizabeth would practice with her swim team. Elizabeth devotes about an hour and a half to her swimming every day. Swimming served as Elizabeth's physical education portion of her schooling. Participation on the swim team also involved weekend trips all around the state. Elizabeth is pleased with her performance on the team. She constantly improves her times and in a two-month period, she took almost sixteen seconds off her former best time in one swimming event.

Along with textbooks, Elizabeth utilizes her computer for information gathering and studying. Elizabeth has CDs with all kinds of programs ranging from statistics to French. She finds these resources very helpful and enjoyable, especially considering the fact that she can work with these programs throughout the day whenever she has free time.

Elizabeth takes an art and a science class outside of her home. These classes usually have about five or six other home schoolers of all ages. These classes are low key and the students really get to know the teacher. Elizabeth enjoys these classes and likes the opportunity to meet new people and interact with kids her own age. Elizabeth's home schooling program is peppered with many outside events and activities and it would be safe to say that Elizabeth spends as much time outside her home as she does in it. Due to this invigorating and interesting program her mother has designed, there is no wonder why Elizabeth has experienced so much success and possesses such a wonderful love for learning.

In Home Schooling, I Can Do the Cool Stuff!

One appealing component of Elizabeth's home schooling program is the flexibility to do some unusual and interesting things. In addition, Elizabeth feels that she can give her full attention and time to the activities in which she is involved. A case in point is the time she spent on the planning and preparing for the performance in her Bat Mitzvah.

Everyone in attendance on that day was amazed at Elizabeth's participation in the ceremony. Along with her compliance to the complex ritual that was required in this event, Elizabeth prepared a one-woman performance where she took on the roles of two characters engaged in dialogue concerning the teachings of her religious studies. The audience was hushed throughout the performance. Elizabeth's performance is something I will always remember for her creative approach to representing two points of view and the level of commitment required for this enriching experience to have taken place. It was truly magical.

Elizabeth commented that she felt good about her performance for her Bat Mitzvah as well as in her part in the community play, The Dybbuk. Elizabeth realizes that these wonderful opportunities would have been difficult, if not impossible, to experience if she had been in school full time.

> *I couldn't have done The Dybbuk and the Bat Mitzvah if I were in school and swimming too, because if I had done that, I would have no time for homework unless I stayed up to twelve o'clock every night. Being home schooled, I have flexibility to do cool stuff. I can take arts in the day and swimming in the afternoon.*

These cool activities became part of Elizabeth's home schooling program where she could rehearse, create, and practice for these events. Learning in home school was connected to these activities and took on special meaning in Elizabeth's life.

Teachers and People and Power

After speaking about the perfect teacher, our conversation drifted to the subject of power dynamics between teachers and parents and children. Elizabeth had some very interesting things to say about her experiences in this regard.

Elizabeth talked earlier about a teacher who would just take over. By this she meant that the teacher would over-talk those around her and take away the students' voices to a certain degree. In this case, the teacher would become somewhat preachy, lecturing to them about what should and should not be done, what was right and what was wrong. This control dynamic would also take place with parents, though in a different form, and would bring the same results: power over others and shaping the environment to her [the teacher's] own design. Elizabeth told a story to illustrate what she was saying.

> *They [some teachers] don't like parents involved. OK, [one year] certain parents didn't like that my mom was helping out the teacher so much, so then they kinda rebelled against my mom. The teacher did nothing to help my mom.*

Elizabeth noticed what was going on among these adults and felt sorry for her mom, who was really trying to help the teacher and the class in general. Elizabeth speculates that the other parents were jealous that her mom and the teacher spent so much time together. In time, the classroom teacher may have felt that she was having to share some of her decision-making power and, ultimately, the power she held as classroom leader was threatened.

In another situation with a teacher, Elizabeth was often placed in the opposing situation of trying to obey her parents' requests and at the same time comply with the sensibilities of her classroom teacher. According to Elizabeth, dialogue with this teacher sometimes took on an unfriendly, authoritative tone.

> *"You don't need your mom to edit everything," and I thought, too bad! She kept it up and said, "You don't need to call your mom on the cell phone." She didn't think that was necessary. We used the cell phone to let her [mom] know we arrived [at school] . . . She [the teacher] wanted to control our lives.*

Elizabeth loved having her mom in school, but with all the things that were going on with the adults, school began to seem tiring. This experience and others like it were some of the main reasons why Elizabeth's family eventually decided to home school.

Relationships in Home Schooling

I asked Elizabeth to talk a little about the people in her life and how home schooling had molded those relationships.

Elizabeth commented that having a mom who is also your teacher is not confusing at all. Aubrey set the precedent years ago when she would follow her children to public school to work as a volunteer. Elizabeth associated learning and schooling with her parent from that early time. Elizabeth commented that she enjoys the time she spends with her dad in the teaching/learning situation. Elizabeth's dad was a history major in college and taught the kids for a time. Elizabeth is very proud of her father and would like to spend more time with him. Elizabeth sometimes needs a break from her brother. Sometimes they fight and bicker. Though Elizabeth does have many fond memories with Jackson, she does need her space from him at times. The structure of her home schooling situation allowed Elizabeth to work alone and in her own space for much of the time if she desired it.

Relationships with other kids are often a subject of discussion when dealing with home school situations. Elizabeth does not feel isolated from her peers because much of her home schooling experiences occur outside of the home with other kids with similar interests.

> *A lot of kids say that they miss kids at school, but I say you can still keep in touch. I have fun with home school and have friends too. A lot depends on your mom and dad and how they teach and how much independence they want to give you. And it depends on you, too.*

Elizabeth realizes that success in home schooling depends on the relationships that are established and maintained among parents, siblings, and friends. What's different about home schooling is that there is more emphasis on relationships with family members than with friends as may not be the case in the public or private school environment.

Elizabeth looks forward to continuing her home schooling for the remainder of eighth grade and possibly into high school. She expresses no reservations about taking alternative measures in earning her high school diploma and continuing on to college.

I wish Elizabeth the best of luck in the future and feel lucky to have recorded her experiences in this home school story.

Chapter Three:
Jackson's Story

Introduction

For Jackson's interviews, I was back in the Watersons' home once again. Jackson greeted me at the door and immediately walked with me into the living room where our discussions would take place. As I came into familiar surroundings, I noticed how quiet the house was. Jackson told me that everyone was away either running errands or working. This wonderfully secure and comforting setting framed our conversations on that beautiful July day.

At the time of the interview, Jackson had just turned thirteen. Jackson is about five and a half feet tall with brown hair and brown eyes. From my acquaintance with him, I have noticed that personal appearance is very important to him. Often Jackson will ask me, "Hey Brian, does my hair look okay?" Of course, it looks great. Jackson is always neatly dressed and takes pride in the way he looks.

Jackson is fascinated with electronics and quite knowledgeable of all the gadgets that have been invented within the last few years. He is constantly talking about his Palm Pilot™, his personal Global Positioning System, and the computer software he uses. This young man is my best consultant in the area of electronic technology. Jackson also has a great sense of humor and is either cracking a joke or up to something unpredictable. He is always willing to share his opinions and engage those around him in conversation. These interviews with Jackson certainly provided me with excellent information about the home schooling experience. Though Jackson appeared to have enjoyed the interview process, I am aware of the time and effort he offered in order to help me with this study. I will be forever grateful to him.

My First Days in School

The first thing Jackson remembered about his schooling was his teachers' reactions to the questions he had. He possessed a genuine interest in knowing how everything worked from an early age.

> *Well, I remember [during my first years in school] that the teacher would say something and tell about the subject, and I would want to know more about it. I would ask a question about it. I kept asking questions relating to what the teacher was saying, but the teacher wouldn't answer me.*

Jackson characterizes much of his public school experiences as frustrating. He feels that teachers in public school want the kids to have a general understanding of the subject matter they teach rather than an in-depth knowledge of the subject. He would have loved to have done more research on the subjects to which he was introduced while in school. He would often follow up on his school studies at home with the help of his mother.

I believe this early habit of extending classroom learning in the home set the stage for full time home schooling when Jackson reached the fifth grade. Jackson and his family realized the limitations of the public school classroom early in their public school experience and initiated measures to provide for him and his sister with home education activities.

Jackson recalled that he was something of a perfectionist up to about the fourth grade. He always felt nervous around the teacher and was concerned that his work would not be good enough. Still, Jackson's work was often used as the example for the other kids in class, which, in a way, added to his feelings of stress and pressure to perform.

> *I always did such good work, that he [the teacher] showed my work to everyone and told the class that this is a good example. I kinda got embarrassed sometimes and I just felt that if I didn't do good enough, or live up to his expectations, I felt that I had failed.*

Jackson remembers his teachers pressuring him to do work over and beyond what he considered to be good levels. These perceived teacher expectations were often accompanied with feelings of sadness, which led to his blaming himself for not working up to his true abilities. Associated with his perfectionist tendencies, he also had to deal with issues of time management. Jackson found himself reviewing and editing his work many times over. His thoroughness often produced negative results in the form of incomplete tests and homework assignments that would at times be turned in late or not at all.

Though Jackson did have to struggle with managing his time wisely and dealing with his perfectionism, he characterized his grades in school as "pretty good." Usually, he was at the top of his class in most subjects. It was not until the fourth grade that he discovered these perfectionist tendencies in himself and started working on strategies to deal with this aspect of his learning and personality profile.

Today, Jackson feels much differently about his work and the approach he takes to complete it. At present, he is "low-keyed" about his learning and feels more comfortable around his teachers. He has also read a book on perfectionism and, as a result, understands why he used to feel stress in the learning environment. Jackson still likes to do his best and sometimes feels the effects of wanting to do a perfect job. He realizes that in order for these tendencies go away, he will have to develop a strategy for dealing with his hypercritical nature in evaluating his own work.

Teachers Are Teachers

During the interview, I asked Jackson to describe the public school climate. He immediately focused on his experiences with the teachers he had and the feelings he received from them.

> *Teachers are teachers. It's hard to explain, but I can just remember doing what I was told. There were teachers who were good and teachers who were not so good. Sometimes they [the not-so-good teachers] were not fair to everybody and you would just have to learn to be a student of that teacher.*

Jackson's impressions of the teachers he had were mixed.

The teachers he favored most possessed a sense of fairness and justice in running the class. He never characterized any teacher as bad, due to the feelings of respect he held for them and the importance of the role they fulfilled. Jackson's approach to dealing with teachers he regarded as not so good was to cope with the demands these teacher placed on their students and try to "live with them."

Jackson spoke at length about his experience with one teacher who favored the girls and treated the boys in class unfairly.

> *I remember once, one of the teachers was very sexist. [This teacher] was on the girls' side all the time. If the girls were naughty, she really wouldn't pay attention, but if the boys were, she would rag on them. During quiet time she would always choose girls to evaluate us, give points, and get things taken away.*

This teacher certainly challenged his concept of right and wrong. Through it all he remained silent, sometimes with tears, and complied with this teacher's class rules. To Jackson, it was more important to adhere to the teacher's rules than to question her sense of fairness. Though he did not like the way this class was run, Jackson learned to live in the environment that was imposed upon him.

Another thing that bugged Jackson was the fact that much of the teacher's time was spent with kids who had behavioral problems and who acted out in loud and disruptive ways. Jackson estimated that at least 35 percent of the students in class needed the teacher's full attention most of the class time.

> *A lot of the teacher's attention was given to the kids that act out. You really wouldn't get the time to spend with*

academics and some fun and other things you need to do in school, and that's a problem.

Jackson commented that he wasted a lot of time every day waiting for the other kids to quiet down. After much deliberation, Jackson estimated that he spent only about two hours a day in activities in which actual academic learning took place.

Jackson also expressed concerns with the other kids in public school. He commented that there were some really nice kids with whom he could talk and have fun, but there were also some kids with whom he had to be very careful. These kids would play pranks like throwing firecrackers at other people and trying to do some really mean things. Though Jackson considers himself to be a sociable person, he is aware that hanging out with kids like these can get him in a lot of trouble. Jackson continues to struggle with this negative peer pressure and is sometimes drawn into situations with others who do not have the best of intentions in mind. He is curious about people and social relationships with his peers and views the social component of school as a form of education that is important to his learning. Jackson truly enjoys the social interactions he has with his peers.

The Home Schooling Experience

According to every family member, Jackson was the one who requested home schooling first. Though he has no recollection of asking for home schooling in the second grade, Jackson does remember that one of his best friends had been a home schooler during this time. To him, home schooling sounded pretty good. His friend spoke about the fun projects he was doing and how he didn't have to sit at a desk all day and do boring worksheets. During the third grade, Jackson does remember asking his mom about home schooling and she said, "No way!" He continued to ask for home schooling until finally, after fourth grade, Aubrey agreed to give it a try for one semester only.

Jackson felt that his parents agreed to home school because they saw very little progress in his learning in school. He also felt that school was "just a day of doing nothing." Jackson really wanted to see some progress in his learning and felt that home schooling was the perfect way to accomplish it.

As fifth grade in home school began, he remembers that one of the first projects he did was writing *The Tribune* with his sister. This was a newspaper for his grandma and grandpa and other relatives who wanted to know about his family's lives and the things they were doing. Jackson and Elizabeth really enjoyed making this newspaper and learned a lot about their family history. To Jackson, this was a great introduction into the world of home schooling.

During that first year, his day in home schooling usually began at 8:25 A.M. He would get ready and begin his studies, usually in math, around 9 o'clock. Jackson worked with a math book called *Saxon Math* that allowed him to work at his own pace in a self-taught style. This book presented problems and examples and then provided answers in the back for checking and grading purposes. Jackson would work on math for about forty-five minutes a day and then move on to his SBM program in science. This science by mail program allowed Jackson to "collaborate" with a scientist from the University of Massachusetts and complete an interactive packet of information that included a series of activities and a final project. At the end of the project, this teacher/scientist would respond to his work by sending notes, suggestions, and encouragement regarding Jackson's work. Jackson also remembers doing with his mom and another home schooled boy a chemistry project involving cabbage in which he learned about bases and acids and the Ph scale. He really enjoyed his exposure to science in that first year of home school.

Some days, Jackson would meet with other home schooled children in parks or in their homes. This would occur mostly on Fridays, once or twice a month for a few hours. Though this group was comprised of mostly younger kids, he admitted that it was fun some of the time. This group of about 11 kids was their designated home schooling group with which he participated in field trips and other special events during the year.

Jackson really enjoyed getting out of the house during the day. Often, he would take the dogs for a walk or spend time rollerblading. Sometimes this walker of dogs would tie the beasts up to his scooter and tour the neighborhood at breakneck speeds. These were some of the most enjoyable moments in his home schooling experience. Jackson considers all of these activities as part of his home school learning.

Another important component of his home school experience was the field trips he and his family would take. Though Jackson can't remember all of the trips, he did remember some of the more interesting ones. He was impressed with the trip to Intel, a behind the scenes look at a violin shop, a two-week trip to Atlanta, Georgia, and a three-week trip to New Zealand. He realized that these golden opportunities could not have been possible if he had been in public school. Leaving school for extended periods of time is almost impossible in regular school. He commented that the trip to New

Zealand was for fun and education. Jackson and his family traveled from Wellington to Auckland, touring both the north and south islands. He commented that the trip was fascinating. They spent their time sightseeing, backpacking, and just doing the tourist thing. He would like to go back at some point, though he realizes that for this to happen, home school is almost mandatory.

Jackson also spoke about the downside of home schooling. As mentioned before, he considers himself to be a social person. Jackson truly missed the social interaction with his peers during his time at home.

> *Sometimes I felt that I just needed to get out of the house. I didn't have enough social time. I mean, I rarely saw my friends. My mom said, "Well, if you're in school you don't see them anyway," but I don't really believe that. If you're in school, there are many opportunities to see people, talk to them.*

It is obvious that along with strong academics, Jackson also sees the need for the social aspect of school. Though he realizes that students usually can't talk during class time, he does find that there are times during the day—lunch, passing in the hall, and before school—when students can talk to other kids and have fun. This is one thing he missed in home school. Jackson commented that it was nice having his sister in home school with him, but she did not fill all of his social needs. At times, Jackson experienced these feelings of isolation in home school.

> *Well, when I think about it, sometimes I get really lonely. And that is the hardest struggle. Lots of people who*

home school feel this way and that's why they go back to school . . . they need people, a kid their own age.

He believes that other home schooled kids feel the same way and that it is natural for kids to be curious about their peers—what interests them and what makes them tick. To Jackson, being in home school removes him from this experience with his peers. He also enjoys having people around that he can talk to and share his feelings with. In addition, he feels that having other kids around gives him a sense of structure, almost like a reality check, which is essential from time to time.

At the beginning of eighth grade, Jackson enrolled in a public charter school where he has experienced success both socially and academically. His most recent report card contains A's and one B. Though he feels accepted by his peers, Jackson has yet to find that one special friend whom the poet Rilke describes as "your prayers answered." Jackson is considering a return to home school due mostly to the low standards in the school curriculum and the fact that the vast majority of students are not serious about the time they spend in school. Jackson feels that the kids are not really there to learn; they are more interested in wasting time, goofing off, and exploring the social aspects of adolescence. Interestingly enough, the major reason he considered this school and his return to public education in general was due to the lack of peer interaction he experienced in home schooling. He is finding out that perhaps it is not the quantity of social interaction in one's life that is important, but rather the quality. He has asked his mom for permission to return to home schooling. When he entered public school last fall, Jackson made a commitment to his family to remain in school for at least one semester.

With the coming of the new year and the next semester, Jackson may well choose to withdraw from public school and return to home education once again.

In the near future, Jackson intends to enroll in either a public or private high school where he can earn the credits he will need for graduation and his high school diploma. Though Jackson realizes that home schooling in high school is more difficult than in elementary or middle school due to the required credits, he knows that it is still possible to achieve a high school diploma. If he decides home schooling is the route he wants to take, he is willing to give the extra effort required for high school completion. His plans for his education and career after high school include attending college as a student of engineering or architecture; then he hopes to secure a job in one of those career areas.

Jackson is unsure about home schooling's effects on his future. He doesn't really feel that home school has changed him, though he does think home schooling has been a positive experience in nurturing his strengths, which he identifies as good attention to detail, mathematics, and sensitivity to other people's feelings.

Considering his strengths and the things he has experienced so far in his young life, I feel that Jackson has a very bright future. I am certain he will realize his dreams.

The Family Politics of Things

Part of Jackson's home schooling program involves interacting with all family members in a spirit of cooperation and the responsibility of taking on chores around the house. For

Jackson, balancing academic work with family responsibilities in his home school sometimes became difficult.

> *Sometimes it felt like I had to do too much stuff because I was home and mom would just walk around and say, "Jackson, I need you to do the dishes." I'd be right in the middle of work. It didn't happen too often, but I didn't like that because it interrupts me . . . I like helping out, but I don't like that scene.*

Jackson realizes that his home school study program includes a family responsibility component. Jackson would prefer to be able to separate his home life from his life in home schooling.

> *Sometimes you want them to be separate [studying and home responsibilities]. Sometimes you just don't want to be in the family politics of things, where you know your sister and your mom are all mad at you. I did not like that about home school.*

He also commented that it was often difficult to interact with Aubrey, who played the major role in his home school education program. Jackson admits it was sometimes difficult to see Aubrey and decide which role she was playing: mother or teacher. Jackson would get mad at things sometimes, but he knew he just had to deal with them. Jackson's dad, Vernon, did share the teaching responsibilities with Aubrey for a while in the beginning of his home school experience, which eased this stress level to some degree. Vernon began to teach the kids history but, after a short time, relinquished the teaching of history to Aubrey.

Jackson comments that in the seventh grade, his mother "kinda backed off," allowing her some personal time to do some things for herself. In a way, Jackson was forced to become a more independent and self-reliant learner. He did not really like the new arrangement of his home schooling program and would have preferred Aubrey to help more in the learning process. Still, Jackson views Aubrey's move away from the home school as positive for his mother but admits to having "mixed feelings" about Aubrey not being there as much as she used to be.

Technology and Home Schooling

As mentioned earlier, Jackson loves all things electronic. I asked him to talk about technology and its part in his home education program.

To Jackson, computers do not occupy a major focus of his home education experience. Most of the time he spends on the computer is when he is typing and word-processing.

> *I mean, if I need some information from the Internet, I might go to my computer, but I usually start with my books. We have some good encyclopedias. I see computers as a multi-media resource. You don't need to use it for all your research needs, and sometimes you can get misleading information on the World Wide Web.*

Jackson and I both agreed that it is possible for truth to become somewhat diluted on the Internet. Anyone can build a web site and say just about anything she/he wants to say. Jackson believes that there is more truth in print, and for him books hold more meaning and are more trustworthy. Jackson gave a wonderful example of how technology attempts to represent the truth but often falls short of its goal. For his Bar

Mitzvah, Jackson was given a Global Positioning System. He has spent countless hours working/playing with it and locating places in his environment.

> *With this program, you can zoom into cities and streets. It will show Solano, Alliso, and Carsile. It also says that we (the company) are not responsible for misleading information. They try to make it the best they can . . . but you never know!*

Jackson realizes the loopholes in much of the technology that exists today, but at the same time he is drawn to it like a moth to the flame. Technology and all that it has to offer is often the catalyst for Jackson's inquisitive nature and certainly plays into the discovery style of learning he enjoys.

I asked Jackson if his mother would allow him to integrate his love for technology into his home school program. He immediately said, "Sure, and she would help you!" If he would choose, Jackson could integrate his love of technology into his program, though he commented that he would still be required to do his regular work. This could be done easily; it just takes tweaking the daily schedule a little to accommodate the new interest. Jackson started a video project that also included work with cameras, but for some reason he never really got into it. He views the ability to include a personal passion or subject in the already existing home school program as a definite strength. Jackson feels that he was given some flexibility to peruse his own interests in his home school setting, but he also feels that he could have been given more chances and support for the inclusion of the things he loves into his program.

Home Schooling Is Not for Everyone

Though home schooling has worked for Jackson and his sister, he would not recommend it to every kid. It takes a special kind of student to benefit fully from home schooling.

> *I just think some people just wouldn't enjoy it, or they wouldn't have enough discipline. You need self-discipline and that is sometimes hard. Doing things without being told, knowing what you need to do, and not procrastinating too much.*

The perfect candidates for home schooling are the families and students who really want to try it. The mom or the adult who will be giving the major part of the instruction will have to be clear about what she expects from her students and what needs to be done. This parent needs to let her children know about everything that will go on in home school. This includes what they will study, how long they will spend in each subject area, what the subject areas will be, and what field trips the students will take during the year. Jackson feels that having this dialogue with the parent/teacher helps.

As far as the kids go, the students should be serious learners who are self-disciplined and who will take on the responsibility for their own learning. Jackson feels that home schooling may not be the best option for kids who don't really want to work and learn. He feels that these kids might abuse their time at home and would be better off in public school where there are definite boundaries and limitations and where discipline is strict. One important part of this equation for successful home schooling is for the parent to make sure the kids will study what they want to learn. Most of the time in public school, students are learning what the teacher wants to teach them or what they are told to teach the kids. In home school, the parent should have the flexibility to teach her children what the kids want to learn. It makes school fun and interesting when you can learn about the things in life in which you are interested. Jackson sums it up by offering his advice to those considering home schooling as a viable option to public or private school.

> *I would tell these people first, the kids should really want to try it. The mom should tell the kids what she expects and what needs to be done and all of the options that would be good.*

It is clear that Jackson regards home schooling as a truly collaborative effort and that each party in the home schooling family should be agreeable to partnership in this educational endeavor. Open communication, the desire to learn on the children's part, and a willingness to share in the curriculum planning stages on the parent/teacher part are what is needed in order for a home schooling program to be successful.

Epilogue to Jackson's Story

During the final stages of this writing, Jackson did withdraw from the public charter school he had attended from the beginning of his eighth grade year and returned to home school with his mother and sister. In his move back to home schooling, Jackson commented that the teachers were not the issue. Jackson stated that the teachers were great and had much to offer the students. Problems that Jackson faced were mostly from other students who did not value learning.

Jackson's experience of waiting for others to assume a learning posture once again arose in which Jackson found himself wasting enormous amounts of valuable time.

In our final interview, Jackson said he was glad to be back in home school with his sister where he could once again work to his full potential on subjects of special interest. Jackson also mentioned the relational dynamic of being home again and felt he had lost something of the closeness that he once had with his family members by being away in school. In the public school environment, Jackson forced himself to deal with many of the complicated social issues that arose. He felt that he had learned a lot about people and, in a strange way, had become a much stronger person as a result of this experience.

Chapter Four:
Vernon's Story

Introduction

My interview session with this last family member, Vernon, Jackson and Elizabeth's father, took place at a medical center in town. In making arrangements for our conversations, Vernon suggested that we meet at times when he was at the hospital on call, during the slow times in the evening when the patients were at rest. I agreed and a few days later I received a call from Vernon asking me to come in during his evening watch. As I entered the medical center and was ushered through a security point, I saw Vernon at the other end of the sterile hall, stethoscope tastefully hanging from his shoulders, garbed in a white lab jacket. He immediately escorted me to his office, past oxygen cylinders, large machines that go ping, tubs of rubber gloves, and racks of operating gowns. Vernon's office was beautifully maintained and decorated with comfortable chairs and a portable waterfall on a bookcase that gurgled calming sounds throughout our conversations. The lighting in his office was indirect and soothing, adding to this relaxed atmosphere. Vernon sat behind his desk and I was positioned in front of him in an overstuffed chair. I believe we both felt comfortable in this quiet, late night setting.

Vernon is in his late thirties and has a very approachable demeanor. I have noticed that when one talks with him, he concentrates on the speaker and listens very intently to what is being said, not wanting to miss a word. Vernon has the unique ability to combine the qualities of seriousness with a strong sense of warmth and trust. I have found through our many interactions together that he is an intelligent and insightful person, willing to share his experiences and knowledge. Vernon's family occupies the center of his life. He takes his role as parent and husband very seriously and, though his job does not afford him the free time he would like, he makes all attempts to be with his family as much as possible.

My feeble attempts to describe Vernon are better left to his own words and descriptions, which have been interpreted throughout the remainder of this text. I hope the reader can capture the essence of this complex man and come to understand and appreciate his insightful comments as I have.

Thinking Outside the Box

Vernon began our conversation by stating that home schooling was not his idea, but rather Aubrey's, who had decided to be at home with the children. He remembered several problems going on in schools during the fourth grade. First of all, Jackson and Elizabeth's teacher was definitely "anti-boy." Both children and Aubrey felt this very strongly. This teacher continually put down Jackson and the other boys in class. Jackson would often come home very defeated and discouraged about school. Secondly, Aubrey, who had been volunteering enormous amounts of time in the classroom, was beginning to feel disrespect from the teacher she had spent so much time supporting. Though Jackson had mentioned home schooling before, Aubrey was the one who brought it up for family discussion and the one who really made it happen. Vernon did not embrace the idea at first and was somewhat skeptical about the whole endeavor.

> *I was really confused. I mean, I could see her point. I just kept worrying, "Oh my god, what does this mean?" It was stressful because I just didn't buy into it and say, "Let's give up on this public school thing," even though I knew, intellectually, that it could work. Aubrey is always one to think outside the box. It made me really nervous.*

Though he could understand every point Aubrey and the kids were making in support of home schooling, Vernon had a struggle with moving outside of the normal conventions of schooling. Vernon was most concerned about the "paper trail" that would be absent from the kids' educational record during the time they were home schooled and could possibly cause problems upon application to high schools and colleges in the not too distant future. What documentation would his children have of their schooling history? How could they compete with other students who had complete school records for every school year documenting their success? In this regard, he felt that his children would be at a definite disadvantage.

Vernon's trepidation with home schooling was also reinforced by his associates at work, many of them doctors, who had never heard of home schooling and who had enrolled their children in elite private schools from very early ages. Many times he felt the social pressures associated with involvement with the alternative educational choice of home schooling, the effects playing themselves out in a kind of devaluing of status in his workplace.

> *Home schooling was so foreign to just about everybody around me that I didn't have anyone to turn to or talk to for support, or to even bounce my fears off of, because it was clearly a lack of understanding from my co-workers. I just couldn't say, "Well, we're doing it our way." I felt that pressure.*

It took Vernon more than a year before he felt comfortable talking about home schooling with his colleagues at work. This new confidence came from recognition of the many great things he was seeing from his children as the direct result of the home schooling. At this point, there was no question in his mind that their home schooling program was superior to the previous public school programs in which the kids were involved.

Thinking back on the whole experience of this move away from public school forced Vernon to criticize himself about the "lack of support" he gave his family at the time. This lack of support was not the result of Vernon's indifference to his family's situation, but rather a result of the confusion concerning what was best for his children and their educational careers. Upon reflection, he realized that the move toward home education turned out to be a positive redirection of energies in bringing meaningful educational experiences to his children on many different levels.

> *What came out of this was Elizabeth and Jackson will maybe think outside the box. You know you don't have to do necessarily what everyone else does because that's what they do, and it's OK to think of other positive ways to solve problems in education or whatever it may be in their life later on . . . not just the popular theory, or the popular answer.*

Vernon's insightful comment takes the reader to another level in his support of home schooling. To him, home education legitimizes the practice of making choices in one's own best interest and also serves as a model for the children to observe and experience, setting the stage for their consideration of alternative possibilities for solving problems later in life.

Family Support for Home Schooling

Some members of both Vernon's and Aubrey's extended families were unsupportive of their decision to home school. Many family members felt they had gone "off the deep end," and expressed serious concerns about the welfare of the children. They were unsupportive to the point of extending guilt to both Vernon and Aubrey, seemingly with the intent of increasing insecurity and anxiety around the issues of appropriate parenting and care for their children. Vernon had hoped his family would support his efforts to home school, but instead the exact opposite occurred.

> *Well, their words would be, "Well, what about the kids and their social skills? How are they going to know what's*

going on with kids at their grade level? How are high schools and colleges going to know anything about what they did?"

These questions went beyond curiosity. Questions were posed in the light of criticism and skepticism. Questions often make statements, and this was certainly the case in these instances. Vernon recognized elements of sincere curiosity, but also saw condemnation, intended harm, and pure ignorance within the comments and questions certain relatives posed. Vernon rationalized these behaviors in a way that focused on human nature, where the first response to lack of understanding is often criticism.

> *I think they [some extended family members] have an insecurity that if someone is doing something that may be better, they criticize them. There are a lot of people who strike out at whatever the source of something different is. So I wonder, with [some of our family members], if this is the case. Insecurity on their part, at the unknown of it. There is no home schooling going on in either of our extended families.*

Again, Vernon characterizes extended family reactions to his family's home schooling endeavors as going beyond mere curiosity due to the non-supportive nature of the comments and questions with which he was confronted. Within this non-supportive position, there also existed elements of resentment for his engagement in a form of alternative education and a parenting style that extended family members perceived as doing nothing more than privileging children. The result of home schooling to them was the production of spoiled children who would be unable to function in society.

Another aspect of Vernon's extended family reaction to home schooling was the influence from the religious culture in which he had been raised. Though the Jewish tradition does embrace the family, they do not, stereotypically, approve of home schooling.

> *A lot of Jewish families, at least American Jewish families, would really push their kids with education, and what that means is a piece of paper, primarily a degree. And so whatever education that you're getting outside of a formal education program is just not good enough. It's foreign to a lot of Jews.*

Vernon believes this attitude can be traced to a time before and during World War II in Europe, when a piece of paper meant everything, life and death at times. It was your defense and identified and measured your worth as a human being. Paper, in its many forms, could prove who you were to the non-Jewish outside world. It was a defense for Jews who were in the minority in Europe and America. Though family does occupy a central position within the Jewish community, home schooling is not valued due to its position outside of the formal school institution and the lack of legitimacy it provides for its participants.

Vernon and Aubrey continue to struggle with this unfortunate extended family dynamic and try their best to be as open and non-judgmental as possible.

Education: The Great Equalizer

I asked Vernon to talk about his own story of education and his parents' attitudes about schooling and parenting.

Vernon's parents were totally bonded to public education,

basically because they were products of the public schools. His parents were immigrants from Russia and Poland who passed through public school institutions and regarded the schools as the great equalizers in American society. To them, once you earned a degree, whether in high school or college, it couldn't be taken away. His parents pushed education hard and considered it to be the number one priority in life, taking precedence over everything else.

Vernon was educated in his neighborhood public schools throughout elementary and middle school and into the one high school in his town. He characterizes his high school experience as wonderful. The school had swimming pools, gyms, art centers, and so much more than what is available to students in the public system today. In fact, his public high school had more to offer than many of the private schools in the area.

In one respect, moving away from the public school system was not difficult for Vernon due to his perception that his family was not giving up all that much. Many of the nearby schools have inadequate facilities and large class sizes. His standard for what was expected in public schools was at a much higher level due to his excellent educational public school environment throughout his life. The move to home school may not have taken place if Vernon and Aubrey had lived in a wealthier school district. Vernon embraces the idea of public school, however he realizes that when the schools consistently fail to meet the needs of students in significant ways and when teachers are not responsive to parent input and participation, alternatives should be considered.

He recognizes teachers as the most important link in affecting the lives of children within the public school system.

Vernon remembers the many wonderful teachers he had, especially during his high school years. The teachers he remembers fondly were all men who taught him math, English, and history in the tenth, eleventh, and twelfth grades. These teachers excelled in getting the most out of each student by focusing on the positive and using respect for classroom control.

> *All I remember is them focusing on the positive. I remember the classes being controlled. I have fond memories and a good place in my heart with all of them, and it was just a good feeling . . . they made you feel good with who you were.*

Though these teachers challenged him in an academic sense, what Vernon remembers most is the affective side of education and the feelings he received as a result of interacting with these teachers. More than twenty years later, he still retains a warm place in his heart for these men and recalls the feelings of self worth generated from the time he spent with them. These same teachers gave other kids these feelings too. Their kindness and concern reached across all races, ethnicities, genders, and social standings within the classroom.

> *These teachers knew me as an individual. They knew my quirks, they knew my pluses, and I'm sure they knew my minuses. They made it known that I just wasn't in class, but I was Vernon, and my guess is that they did it with a lot of kids, not just the "smart kids." And I actually think that's a sign of a great teacher. When a teacher can make a kid feel good, the kid's gonna like the teacher.*

In this statement, Vernon has elevated his thoughts from his personal experience with these teachers to a more global position where kindness and concern for all students becomes the issue. He has identified fairness and mutuality as important components for effective teaching.

Vernon also mentioned a high school teacher with whom he was less than enamored. This young teacher was mean spirited and practiced reverse discrimination in her interactions with her students. If she perceived a student as financially in need or one with poor study skills, she tended to privilege them. Conversely, students she perceived as upper or middle class would be marginalized. What Vernon remembers most is that he hated going to this woman's class. Upon leaving it, he frequently had feelings of being put down and somehow guilty of some crime. He never really figured out what his crime was except that he was a serious student from a family who supported his academic endeavors and expected him to be a high achiever.

Vernon's parents were very serious about his education and they encouraged him throughout his schooling, from the elementary grades, high school, college, and into graduate school.

> *I guess I would say, up to about the age of thirty, which was about ten years ago, just everything was education. It was one level of education to another. Public school, secondary school, college, thinking beyond college, thinking about medical school, beyond medical school, thinking about the medical training program, and the residency. None of that was over until thirty, non-stop formal education. So getting educated in a non-formal setting was out of my mindset.*

Vernon's concept of education, shaped by the values given to him by his parents and subsequently by his own experiences, was vastly different than the values and educational approach possessed by many home school advocates, his wife and children included. In coming to terms with making decisions in his children's best interests, Vernon had to take a serious look inside and determine if his values regarding education would meet the needs of his children.

Looking back on his life, Vernon has regrets about "staying on the straight and narrow," where education and work were the driving forces of his experiences.

> *I wanted to bury myself in the middle of Nepal or somewhere. Start in Katmandu and walk. My parents said, "Stay on the straight and narrow, get your degree, and then decide what to do." I think it's a great idea to not do what I did.*

What proved difficult for Vernon was, upon completing his residency program and turning thirty, all of a sudden there was no more straight and narrow path to be found. His world opened up to him with a plethora of opportunities. These new choices presented him with an uneasy feeling he had seldom experienced before, causing a certain degree of depression and confusion. He was used to walking that straight path from one place to another in an ordered sequence. Now that his journey had come to an end, turning points presented him with the difficult task of choosing one from the many available.

Vernon recalls that much of his self-concept was tied up in his school performance. Vernon felt that much of the approval and affection he received from his parents was contingent on his performance in school. He commented that, in a way, he hoped the dynamic of conditional love he felt from his parents during this time was not real and that their reactions to his successes in school were born from their genuine concern for his welfare.

Vernon's personal experiences in education and the values given to him by his parents certainly were instrumental in the serious questioning of home schooling he undertook. Progressing through school in non-traditional and non-formal ways was alien to Vernon, who only wanted the best for his children. Home schooling proved to be a problem for him in many ways. However, due to his abilities to adapt his thinking and accept new ways of education, his family was able to proceed with a very positive home schooling program that enriched the lives of all family members.

The Epiphany: Home Schooling Can Really Work!

When Vernon reviewed current classroom practices in public schools, he commented that classroom space in their town seemed smaller and the student class sizes bigger, with less control of student behavior and learning. From his exposure to the work Jackson and Elizabeth had done, he also felt that the expectations for learning had been drastically reduced and watered down. This realization of current conditions in schools served as the catalyst for his new thinking and new approaches for education for his children. When he saw Aubrey and the kids going on field trips to really interesting sites, like the biosphere, camping trips, skiing trips, and local museums, he began to see learning in a totally different light.

> *When Aubrey and the kids were able to just get up and go somewhere, and use that as a stimulus for learning, I saw the value in it and thought, "Hey, that could really work!" Looking at travel as a form of education as opposed*

to education consisting of what you do in the classroom and at your desk—now those were the things that kept hitting me over and over.

It took Vernon at least the whole first year of home schooling before he had a full understanding of the true impact of home schooling and the degree to which it was fulfilling the educational needs of his children. He came to the understanding that education was everywhere and that education was in everything.

You know, it'd be a field trip to a radio station, or to the mayor's office, anything, anywhere, and you suddenly realize that the opportunity to learn is always there. And you don't have to do it with chalk, which was my mind, or on paper. Sometimes just living through it means a lot.

Vernon gave a wonderful example of what he meant when he said that learning is everywhere and in everything. During their home schooling, the kids took a field trip to a violin shop where they were given a demonstration on how violins are made. Throughout this process Jackson learned that glue was a very important part of the whole process. This got him interested in glue itself, where it came from, and how it was made. This natural flow of the mind making connections to seemingly unrelated ideas is the natural way a child's mind works and something that we as parents and educators do not reinforce or value. We like to organize learning into a form that we perceive as straight and linear. The bending and reshaping of ideas from the natural learner is often not tolerated in the classroom setting. Imbedded in this flow, as Vernon described, are the possibilities for authentic learning and the acquisition of true knowledge. Jackson and Elizabeth's home school education focused on this process of learning and capitalized on teachable, learnable experiences as much as possible.

The minor epiphany he experienced in regard to the ubiquitous nature of learning provided the foundation for Vernon's embrace of home schooling. The academic gains his children were making in the home school environment were hard to ignore, and the inclusion of affective education components had helped to restore the children's love of learning, as well as to foster the parent/child relationship that his family valued.

Thoughts on His Children

I asked Vernon to describe his children to me and talk about the possible effects home schooling has had on them.

Vernon viewed both Elizabeth and Jackson's former school experiences as playing a very big part in the lives and personalities they have today. His children's identity and the way he perceives them as learners are shaped by school in similar ways to how his parents perceived him. His children's strengths, weaknesses, and special abilities are in part defined by their performance in school and their ability to adapt to the school setting. Vernon also painted a picture of his children that presented them as multifaceted individuals with the ability to adapt to different environments and situations.

> *School has definitely played a part in who they are, but there's a musical part of them, and a curiosity part of them. There's a fun part of them, and a swimming part of them. I just see them as complicated people, not as a standard, one size fits all.*

Vernon characterizes his children as "people." He regards them as separate individuals who deserve as much respect and consideration as any adult. It is obvious that he truly loves his children and has a desire to be able to see deep inside of them in order to fully understand their true nature.

In describing Jackson, Vernon jokingly commented that Jackson, and Elizabeth too, were characters. Jackson is persistent, incredibly bright, and naturally curious. Jackson can provide exquisite detail on any subject in which he is interested. Jackson has wonderful powers of concentration and also is able to switch from one subject to the next in perfect flow, connecting seemingly unrelated ideas into his dialogue. Jackson's preschool teacher said it best when she told Vernon, "Jackson is a guy who marches to the beat of his own drum." Vernon commented that there's no question that Jackson possesses certain influences that affect his behavior. Jackson also has the courage and conviction to follow that drumbeat, sometimes to the degree that it marches him in a direction that is not in his own best interest. Often attempts to persuade Jackson to redirect his energies produce resistance to change in what Vernon considers to be a wise direction.

Vernon characterizes Elizabeth as having a gentle spirit, but also a confidence that makes her strong and determined.

> *Elizabeth is a peacemaker. She's musical. She's creative. She is able to reach a goal no matter what it is. She can see the forest through the trees, she gets the big picture, and that's the real strength she has.*

Vernon went on to talk about Elizabeth's incredible sense of logic, her ability to size up a situation, understand what needs to happen in order to get a job done, and solicit the assistance needed for task completion. In addition, she has an unbounded love for animals and a wonderfully playful attitude.

From these descriptions it is obvious that Vernon not only knows his children well, but also has the desire to understand them. This notion was reinforced when I sat in the audience during Jackson and Elizabeth's Bar and Bat Mitzvah and heard Vernon talk about his children. During his presentation, Vernon focused on each child, sang their praises, and then offered his love to them. This display of public affection, seldom seen from a father to his children, made a lifelong impression on me as to the sacred nature of the parent/child relationship and the strength that resides within the core of true love for another. This time it was my turn to experience the moment of epiphany.

The Home Front

As a pre-adolescent, Vernon began to get the feeling that one day he would have to leave his father and mother's home and make his own way in life. This feeling of separation from his parents came at a very young age. His brothers sensed this feeling of separation from their parents as well. Vernon commented that he hopes Elizabeth and Jackson do not ever feel this way and know in their hearts that they will always have a home with him and Aubrey. He believes that home education has reinforced his ideas about family solidarity and strengthened the bonds he has with Aubrey and the children.

Though these family bonds have been strengthened, they have been done so through many stressful times and struggles in dealing with individual personalities, perspectives, and desires. In addition, Aubrey is often preoccupied with her home school program, having a constant internal dialogue asking if she is doing the right thing. What should the kids be doing? Is her teaching effective or not? Vernon realizes that everything has its drawbacks, but for the most part, home schooling really brings the family together.

Vernon explored the area of his relationship with Aubrey and the children in the context of their home schooling experience. In retrospect, many of the problems and confrontations he and Aubrey had could have been avoided if they had communicated more effectively. At the beginning, Vernon was uncertain about the whole idea of home schooling. He had his own biases and identified the whole home schooling movement with Christian fundamentalists, of whom he wanted no part. Vernon's identity came from his strong Jewish cultural background, which did not support a home schooling ideology. He knew there were problems with the public schools, however he pondered if home schooling was the best choice for dealing with his children's educational needs. When Aubrey and the kids began home schooling, Vernon was confused and uncertain about what was happening with his family. This initial move into home schooling proved stressful to both Vernon and Aubrey.

> *I didn't just give carte blanche support to Aubrey. I didn't say, "I trust in what you are doing, and I'm sure everything will go well." So I would passively and actively say or not say things. But my actions would make known that I was having difficulty or stress with what was going on. And it would create tension.*

Aubrey and Vernon did not have a smooth transition in their move away from public school to home schooling.

However, through constant discussion and compromise, the family members began working together in a common effort to build positive bonds.

The positive bonds that were created showed themselves during Jackson and Elizabeth's Bar and Bat Mitzvah. This ceremony and its preparation was regarded as a family effort where the structure of home schooling played the important part of allowing for the time and place for family members to come together. This shared time and the close bonds that were created in connection with the Bar and Bat Mitzvah were made quite obvious on that Saturday morning in June when each family member expressed their feelings of love and connection to the other.

This ceremony and the display of emotions connected to it within this family were quite extraordinary, something I had never witnessed before. For me, the epiphany came with the realization of how disconnected I was from my parents and siblings. Taking a reflexive stand, I realized on this day the importance of trying to make connections with my wife and my daughter and enacting efforts in securing the bonds with them that make life worth living.

Others in the audience expressed similar feelings of amazement with both children's performances to Vernon and Aubrey after the ceremony.

> *A couple of people from Aubrey's family said, "You know, every kid does great with their Bar and Bat Mitzvah, they rise to the challenge, but there was a unique spark behind Jackson and Elizabeth." It [home schooling] allowed them to go, what I would say, that one step further, one step deeper, in what they were able to accomplish and communicate.*

This was only one example that illustrates the power home schooling has had on this family's relationship building, as well as on the deep educational experiences which evolved as a result of its structure. The structure Vernon speaks about also enabled the family to take camping trips and field trips together. Vernon has fond memories of the little trips he and his family took together and looks back with regret at not having taken more.

Vernon regards his desire to spend time with his children as somewhat atypical to the average American values of parenting. He sees and hears about parents who are "kicking their kids out," not in a physical sense, but in an emotional one. He has talked to parents who can't wait for their children to leave home so they can have their own lives back. To him, his children are his life. He is tied to them and Aubrey through the concept of mutuality where his well-being depends on the wellness of all other family members.

Bringing Home into the School

In Vernon's opinion, the first thing we need to do in bringing the feeling of home into the schools and therefore improving them, is to limit the student class size to no more than fifteen children. As classrooms are now, with as many as thirty children, it is impossible for the teacher to get to know each student in an authentic way. Even with smaller class sizes, it would take a talented teacher with the help of a full time volunteer to meet the academic and social/emotional needs of the students in the class. Vernon admits that obviously this would almost double the capital investment of government in education, however the results would well justify the expenditure by nurturing individuals who have positive self-images and a sense of belonging and who can act in civically competent ways.

Secondly, bringing a sense of family and home into the schools would endorse a system of consequences for student action and inaction. The embrace of the family concept in schools would include parents, teachers, administrators, and students in a positive partnership for the betterment of the local school community and all its members. At present, Vernon perceives the schools and parents in a divorced relationship with one another, each party blaming or passing the responsibility to the other.

> *There has to be consequences for the kids in school, where the principal meets with the parents and they say, "This is the problem. How are we all going to solve it?" Too often I see parents saying, "It's the school's job to educate them. It's not mine."*

On the positive side, Vernon remembers Jackson and Elizabeth's third grade teacher who insisted that at least one parent participate in classroom meetings throughout the year. This also meant that parents were not only invited into the classroom during the day, but also expected to be frequent members of the classroom. This third grade teacher was a true leader who desired a strong partnership with all stakeholders.

> *She said, "You guys, you parents, are part of the education this year; it's not just me teaching the kids." And she really got not just parent involvement of being told what to do, but she would also listen to parents. She was strong willed and had her ideas, but it was the way . . . she made parents feel important, and I think that that's a big key!*

The big key to Vernon was the positive relationship that the teacher initiated with the parents from day one. She positioned herself as the classroom leader in a way that included parents and gave them a voice that was valued in authentic ways. This was not just lip service; she was sincere in her desire and efforts to include parents in the students' educational experiences.

The third component of making the home school connection was focused on the issues of parenting even before the child came to school. Vernon felt that parenting was paramount to everything that went on in school. Parenting should reinforce the idea of respect for others in the world and guide children to an understanding of the boundaries of appropriate behavior. He gave an example of a crowded school hallway during a class change. Kids were moving through the hall, roughhousing in both physical and verbal ways but knowing at some point that there was a line that you just didn't cross. Most kids had this awareness, but some did not. The kids who did not have this sense had to learn where these boundaries fell, often at the expense of other children and adults who were forced into being their mentors through painful personal experiences. Vernon believed these children had never been taught the subtle art of boundary drawing.

> *I just think that a lot of kids with absent parents . . . I'm not saying single parents, I'm saying absent parents, which to me might mean a two doctor parent family, who doesn't set limits. It's not a money issue; it's parents being involved with their kids from an early age. What I see with gangs is kids who have grown up in houses without limits. They're searching for limits, kids want them, they feel secure with limits.*

Vernon is a believer in limits and making these limits known. His concept of boundaries is not draconian in any way. In fact, Vernon advocated having children involved in the formation of community limits on behavior. Furthermore, all stakeholders should adhere to these limits: students, teachers, administrators, and parents alike. Being on the same page in terms of guidelines and expectations for behavior would certainly be helpful in creating a home atmosphere in school. To Vernon, the difficult part of this equation was drawing these boundaries to include all community voices and administering this behavior code in a fair and equitable manner.

An Investment in Our Children

One of the most difficult hurdles to overcome when a family decides to home school is dealing with the realization that one parent has to give up a paycheck or career in order to be home with his/her children. It's almost like trading investments—our financial future for the future of our children—and in a larger sense, our society. Vernon commented that some people might look at home schooling as an elitist activity due to the low percentage of families who are engaged in it and because of the fact that it is removed from mainstream educational practices. Vernon believes that home schooling will always remain on the fringes of educational practices and only involve a small percentage of the American public. His reasons for this statement include his perception that parents do not really desire to spend time with their children. Furthermore, the children, through acculturation from the parents, don't really want to spend time with their parents. The claim that some people make about elitism and home schooling and the fact that only professional people can afford to practice it is totally unfounded. In Vernon's opinion, that excuse serves as a smokescreen for larger issues.

> *I would argue that we can all afford to home school. It's a matter of budgeting how much money we are all going to spend. What size house, what kind of car we want? So I think both people don't have to work. If they think they do, then they're not right for home schooling.*

Some home schooling families with which Vernon is familiar would have preferred to send their children to private school as a response to the poor learning environment in public school, but due to the high tuition, chose to home school instead. To these families, private school wasn't an option. The better compromise was for one parent to exchange her/his salary and job or career for work at home with the children. This was the case with Vernon and Aubrey. They could have chosen a more luxurious life if Aubrey had continued to work. However, the choice they made was to give up their consumer potential for their children's education and development. More than anything else, to home school or not to home school is a matter of individual choice and based on the values that are important to each family.

In Vernon's work as a medical specialist, he deals with a wide range of people and families from a variety of cultural and socioeconomic backgrounds. He has delivered babies from girls as young as thirteen years old to mothers in their fifties who have had many children before. He has concern for many of them who pass through the hospital doors in regard to their ability to parent the children they bring into this world.

I have seen many parents who I don't think were fit to be parents. I don't think it matters if they work or if they don't work. It's the fact of are they going to invest in their kids. And it's not if they're going to be perfect parents, because none of us are perfect parents. It's the fact that they are willing to invest in their kids.

Vernon estimates that the majority of deliveries in which he is involved are products of a sexual union in which there was no planned desire to produce children at all.

At least three out of four pregnancies occur [simply] because sex occurred, not because they [the parents of newborn infants] are looking and planning and thinking of holding a baby, a toddler, a child, a teenager, and the subsequent adult child.

To Vernon, it is the simple truth and a sad commentary that our society really doesn't value children to the degree it should. Many parents do not regard time spent with their children as high on their priority list and would rather put up with inadequate educational programs in public school than bring their children back to the home where they can care for them. For the teacher in public school, trying to create a sense of family in the classroom is nearly impossible, especially when partnered with uninvolved parents who are unconcerned about the school experience for their children.

In the classroom, no matter how good the teacher is, they're still not family. Those three teachers I talked about earlier were also parental figures; they made me feel important. Most teachers don't have time for that, and it's not the reality of having thirty kids and the demands that are placed on them [the teachers]. And the bottom line is they are not their children.

Vernon's connection with those three teachers was certainly a wonderful experience, though perceiving meaningful relationships from only three out of the scores of teachers with whom he interacted seems inadequate. Bringing elements of home into the school would certainly help in making that personal connection between adults and children. To Vernon, that connection can only be bridged through cooperation, effort, and a true desire for a sense of home on the part of all stakeholders.

The True Beauty of Home Schooling

To Vernon, one of the benefits of home schooling is the attention that can be given to the affective side of education, particularly in the area of self-esteem.

> *I'll tell you, the true beauty of home schooling is fostering the development of self-esteem. If the parent is smart enough to allow the child's self-esteem to flourish, that child will be able to make it in just about any other environment. Self-esteem is that important and it is a huge positive to home schooling.*

To Vernon, in the typical classroom, there might be five out of thirty students who have a healthy self-image. The other twenty-five are still dealing with issues of self-esteem and searching for their place in the social context. Students who have already developed this perspective have a great advantage over those who still deal with the discovery of boundaries within social relationships. In the home schooling environment, parents and students can work on these issues at a personal level and construct the learning environment to meet the individual needs and learning style of the student. In Jackson and Elizabeth's case, attention to the learning environment included activities of individual interest at home as well as outside of the home with other children, which included music, art, and swimming. These activities were designed in consideration of the children's interests with teachers who were selected, not assigned, and who were enthusiastic about working with the children.

Vernon voiced two cautions about the home school situation in regard to conditions of isolation sometimes experienced by home schooling children.

> *I think if a kid is only in their own house and is not around other kids, I think there's a potential problem for that kid and his understanding of the world.*

Vernon believes that kids who have never been exposed to large group settings in school may not possess the skills to give and receive social cues that are such an important part of our daily communication. In Elizabeth and Jackson's circumstance, since they had attended public school for more than four years, they had been exposed to the social signals that were enacted by their fellow students. Due to the exposure of peer communication signals, Jackson and Elizabeth could easily negotiate and interpret their meanings.

A large part of school is socialization. Education hasn't changed much since the 1920s when we had a country full of immigrants who needed to learn the ways and customs of the people of the United States. Public schools during this time served society well in their attempts to reach out to those individuals who needed assistance in socialization and the eventual assimilation process that would place them squarely in the mainstream of American society. But today, American society has changed and moved past the needs it so desperately had in the past. Though society has changed, schools haven't.

Issues of socialization are often raised in regard to home school children and their ability to engage with other members in the real world. Vernon is concerned with questions regarding the nature of the real world. Is the real world the public school classroom where children are required to sit behind a desk with other individuals with whom they may not desire to associate? Vernon answers his own question.

> *In the real world, we talk about social skills. How often are we forced to be around people we don't want to be around? I think many of us choose jobs that we were attracted to because there are people we want to be around. I guess my criticism to the social thing is, who's to say you learn that in school? People assume that when they're in school, they're getting social exposure to the school of hard knocks. I think that's BS.*

In the real world, we make choices. As adults, if we find a neighbor or co-worker who displeases us, many times we can minimize our contact with that person by avoiding or reducing our exposure to her/him. Kids in school are expected to put up with the people they find offensive every day with little choice or control of their contact with them. Is this the real world?

To Vernon, the beauty of home schooling lies in the ability to make choices for his children and to assist them in directing their lives to maximize their skills, abilities, and interests. Most of all, the beauty of home schooling lies in the bonds that are built between parent and child in their lifelong journey together. Vernon believes that home schooling is not a political statement or an exercise in anti-democratic rhetoric, but rather a reflection of true democracy in the expression of opinion through action. Where else could home schooling exist than in a true democratic system where people's values and rights to their own opinions are upheld? Vernon will continue to advocate for his right and the right of others to home school. He regards this form of alternative education to be extremely important and hopes that home schools may one day be as accepted as public and private schools are. What a truly wonderful scenario it would be if public schools, private schools, and home schools would cooperate to provide infinite possibilities for meeting the needs of our children in American society. This dream for the future would certainly include a strong consideration for diversity.

Section Two: Reflection

Chapter Five:
The Emergent Themes

Themes that emerged from this study were created by the voices of all participants and should be considered central to the representation of their home schooling experiences. These areas of mutual concern were generated from the participants' experiences and reflect *their* issues, *their* concerns, and *their* ideas about home schooling. Research questions I entertained were used to inform the research, not guide it.

Our Identity

All participants voiced concern with issues of identity as they transitioned into home schooling practice from the public school environment. These identity issues took a different form from person to person. Each individual provided an insightful portrayal of her/his own perspective.

Aubrey's personal identity was reshaped upon the births of

Elizabeth and Jackson and her return to home for their care. Aubrey made the choice to withdraw from the work force at the cost of her career to instead assume the role of a non-working mother, a role that society devalues. This move back to the home forced Aubrey to reevaluate the importance of her role as mother/caregiver and adjust her thinking to suit her needs and value system rather than basing her identity on the sometimes shallow view society possesses. Working through this identity process and struggling with her own ego led Aubrey to the realization that the time she spent with her children had been a wonderful gift and one she felt fortunate to have experienced. Aubrey's contemporary female friends wanted no part of this homeward move due to their perceptions that being caught back in the home again would place them in financially subservient roles. According to Aubrey, this identity crisis was one of the major impediments to parent support of home school practice. Many women desired to see themselves as financial contributors who were legitimized by their bi-monthly paycheck, regardless of the amount on the dollar line.

Vernon also had identity issues with his family's move away from public schools. Having been brought up in a family and culture that valued public education, his move toward home schooling seemed almost unnatural. Though he understood and agreed with the points his family made about the benefits of home schooling, Vernon felt a strong degree of detachment from this idea that left no paper trace of his children's educational experiences. Extended family members and co-workers also did not support Vernon's move to home schooling. Family members perceived Vernon and Aubrey as partners in poor parenting who over-privileged their children. Vernon's identity at work also suffered due to co-workers who found home schooling alienating and foreign and who either enrolled their own children in public school or private school. Identity issues concerning his role as parent, husband, and son played heavily on Vernon's self-perceptions and identity. It was not until a year later that he felt comfortable talking about home schooling with colleagues at work and giving his immediate family the support they needed in their home schooling efforts.

The children in the study provided a much different perspective into the identity issues that accompanied their move to home schooling. Elizabeth considered herself to be a very good student who could make friends easily and succeed in the public school environment. Her removal from the public school classroom altered her identity from a contributing classroom member to an independent learner at home. How would Elizabeth view herself as a learner in this new home classroom? Would she feel success at home in the same way she did in public school? Certainly Elizabeth took a risk by entering home schooling. Elizabeth's own identity was based around success in learning rather than being stereotyped with home schooling kids who were often viewed by others as "nerdy" or social misfits. Elizabeth's parents characterized her as confident and secure in both academic and social settings. Due to these personal qualities and her strong work ethic, Elizabeth's success in the home school setting was almost guaranteed. Within a few weeks of her entrance into home schooling, Elizabeth realized the tremendous academic gains she was making and found joy in the process of learning and discovery. Elizabeth continues to home school and enjoys the success she experiences.

Like Elizabeth, Jackson also derived his identity from his academic prowess. Jackson viewed himself as a capable student who enjoyed the pursuit of learning. Initially, Jackson was the family member who requested home schooling. Moving back to the home for education was very natural for him and did not prove difficult in any way. Later on in his home schooling career, Jackson did begin to question his identity as a home schooler as a result of the external social reinforcers he experienced. He often picked up subtle messages from community members who perceived and stereotyped him as a typical home schooler who would be better off in public school like "normal kids." These perceptions were heightened by his own desire to be with his peers in school and the feelings of isolation that sometimes accompanied his home schooling experience.

In many ways, the children in the study had an easier time making the transition from public school to home school. Their identity was not particularly tied up in their learning environment, but rather in the academic gains they were making. For Elizabeth, math was self-identified as the subject that grounded her, where music and language arts served as the areas of identity for Jackson. The parents in the study experienced much more challenging issues of identity in their transition to home schooling than the children. Both parents felt the negative social pressures that sometimes accompanied home schooling families. This pressure emanated from extended family members, friends, co-workers, and the public education community.

All family members shared the common identity as thinking people who valued the freedom of choice and the independence to structure their lives to suit their needs. An element of courage was also present within their concept of identity. Courage was required to be able to think outside the box in the consideration of home schooling as an educational option. Courage was also needed to put their thoughts into practice despite the negative social cues they received. Home schooling in this light proved to be a truly transformative experience for this family's members and, in many ways, made them stronger.

Building Relationships

The building of relationships and the importance of the bonds that were created within the context of the home schooling experience were important themes that emerged from this study. For Aubrey, maintaining a positive relationship with her children was paramount in her role as a mother. As the children progressed through public school, she began to see her children separating from her emotionally and showing signs of embarrassment with her displays of affection. When the children began home schooling in the fifth grade, Aubrey recognized some dramatic changes in their behavior. As their year in home schooling evolved she found that her children were no longer afraid to love her and show affection. Aubrey witnessed the return of the closeness they once shared when they were younger. The kids would now "cuddle" with her when they spent time reading together. To Aubrey, home schooling provided the framework for building the positive bonds that she felt were essential to the children's emotional development and her development as well.

Vernon's view of home schooling and the bonds that were built as its result were not as clearly defined as Aubrey's. Vernon was somewhat skeptical of home schooling due primarily to his own educational background and the reinforcement he received from his family on the importance of formal institutionalized education. The move to think outside the box came hard for Vernon and it was not until at least a year into home schooling that he began to support his family's efforts in meaningful ways. The issue of relationships played a dual part in Vernon's participation with home schooling. On one hand, home schooling drew him away and, on the other, it bonded him to the significant people in his life. In regard to certain family members, home schooling tended to alienate Vernon and affect his relationships with these people in negative ways. These people regarded Vernon's home schooling endeavors as a product of poor parenting and the over-privileging of his children. Vernon received little or no support from these relations. Their reaction to home schooling was due in part to their view that home schooling functions outside of the formal school institution and therefore lacks legitimacy. Though the concept of family and the bonds that tie members together was an important part of Vernon's cultural background, home schooling was not valued by his extended family. Many co-workers also did not offer support or encouragement for Vernon's home schooling efforts. In both instances, home schooling had a negative effect on the previous relationships he had established.

In terms of strengthening bonds, home schooling provided the means to reconnect with his children and spouse in meaningful ways. This realization came only after deep reflection and readjustment of the educational values he held. Like Aubrey, Vernon witnessed positive changes in his children's behavior, both academically and emotionally. Vernon's connection to his children, evidenced during his presentation at the children's Bar and Bat Mitzvah, was deepened by the home schooling experience in which he and his family were engaged.

The family's journey into home schooling was not necessarily smooth. During the initial stages of educating at home, Vernon and Aubrey would often have differences of opinion resulting in serious discussions. In retrospect, Vernon felt that the majority of confrontations could have been avoided if he and Aubrey had developed better forms of communication. After working through the philosophical and practical workings of home schooling, Vernon came to realize the power of this alternative form of education and the positive bonds that were created with his immediate family.

Elizabeth addressed the concept of relationship in the context of the educational process itself and the teachers she had throughout her public school and home schooling experiences. She recalled several public school teachers who were more interested in controlling classroom power than in developing caring relationships with students. Though relationship building does not preempt the importance of a teacher's ability to transmit knowledge, Elizabeth does recognize it as an important component of teaching. Elizabeth commented that she seldom experienced a teacher, other than her mother, who combined the ability to teach with the sense of care. Elizabeth felt that her mother pushed her and challenged her in kind and gentle ways. Elizabeth trusts her mom and realizes that Aubrey only wants the best for her.

This trust was developed from an early age when Elizabeth would often return from school in need of additional instruction and call on her mom for help. She felt that her mom did a wonderful job of teaching her the things she needed to know. Today, Elizabeth enjoys the time she spends with her mother in home schooling and regards the many levels of interaction with her as enriching and important.

Jackson's involvement with relationships in regard to home schooling is another story worth telling. As mentioned before, Jackson was the first family member to advocate home schooling. His initial desire to home school was born from his experiences with classmates and certain teachers, who, for the most part, would frustrate him and waste his time. Jackson's self-concept and identity were grounded in his performance in school and in the high standards he set for himself. Jackson found it hard to develop close relationships with classmates who also valued learning. Throughout his school experiences, Jackson has had a love/hate relationship with other kids. His moves in and out of home schooling and public school were motivated by the expectations for relationships he desired to establish. In the home school environment, Jackson often felt lonely and longed for the exposure to peers where the adolescent relationships he entertained would somehow help him through this difficult period of growing up. On his return to public school, Jackson was confronted with the social limitations of his peers. Unable to find friends with whom to share new relationships and armed with the new insights gained from his exposure to his peers, Jackson is now ready to return to home schooling where he may once again focus on his academics. Jackson is suffering from "the grass is always greener on the other side" syndrome accompanied by his true desire to form relationships with his peers.

Jackson also experienced difficulties in his relationship with Aubrey in her shared role as mother and teacher, finding it difficult at times to discriminate between the dual positions she held. Still, working through this struggle, Jackson recognized his mother's good intentions and maintained a positive relationship with her.

It's Not Elitism, It's About Independence and Choice

What was perceived as elitism by many people who criticized home schooling was confused, in Aubrey's opinion, with the sense of independence that comes with it. What was gained from home schooling was the independence to pursue learning experiences that were meaningful to the children. Home schooling meant following her family's own agenda in lieu of the public institution's. It was also about flexibility and finding learning opportunities in everything around you. Aubrey found this feeling of independence exciting and did everything she could to nurture it. Most of all, home schooling was about choice. If people felt they could not afford to home school their children, they shouldn't choose this educational option. In her case, she and Vernon decided it was better to relinquish one person's income in order to provide a nurturing environment for the children. Home schooling was the action associated with a parent's value of the importance of the relationship in her children's lives.

In one section of chapter five, Aubrey attempted to deconstruct the word elitism and came up with an important component inherent in this term. Within the context of educational elitism rests the element of choosing. Aubrey commented that she chose home schooling; it did not choose her. This wonderfully insightful distinction between being chosen and choosing placed the practice of home schooling squarely outside of the accepted definition of elitism.

On the same subject, Vernon commented that one of the

most difficult hurdles to overcome when deciding to home school was dealing with the reality that one parent had to give up a career. When the decision was made to home school, it was very much like trading investments: a short-term financial future for the children's future. Vernon does perceive that society's opinion of home schooling is somewhat elitist in nature, though senses that the application of this label on home schooling practice is a smokescreen to larger issues. Vernon argued that, in regard to financial concerns, all could home school if the desire were there. He felt it was a matter of budgeting the family income and expenditures. More than anything else, he felt home schooling to be a matter of individual choice and the reflection of the values that parents identify as important.

Both parents spoke about the flexibility and independence they experienced while home schooling. During the home school day, Aubrey took advantage of community events and exposed the kids to all kinds of learning opportunities both near and far. One aspect of home schooling that provided Vernon with the epiphany he needed in order to understand that home schooling could work was his recognition of the incredible learning that was going on in association with the field trips his family took. The independence provided by the home school schedule allowed Jackson and Elizabeth to peruse in depth the subjects they had a desire to learn about. During her interview, Elizabeth commented how happy she was that she could study anything she wanted. Having a voice in her own learning provided her with a sense of ownership of which she certainly took advantage. Jackson also appreciated the independence he had in the home school environment in regard to his love of music and the time he had to compose and practice. This flexibility would have been impossible in the public school setting. Jackson realized and expressed the advantages of home education in regard to the incredible flexibility he experienced in home schooling.

A good example of the independent and flexible nature of home schooling was provided when Elizabeth and Jackson performed at their Bat and Bar Mitzvah. During part of the ceremony, each child appeared on stage where they demonstrated their unique talents. The audience was hushed for both performances, surely realizing the gifts these children were presenting and aware of the incredible time and effort that went into the preparation of their performances. All participant family members commented that their involvement in this ceremony, to this degree, would have been impossible had the children not been home schooled. Jackson and Elizabeth had incorporated their religious studies in their home school program where learning became meaningful to them and also served to strengthen the bonds of all family members.

The Perfect Teacher

All family members spoke about their experiences with the teachers in their lives. Vernon in particular spoke with fondness about three high school teachers who encouraged and inspired him and brought out his best qualities and abilities. He connected with these teachers due to their willingness to know each student in their classes. In these high school classrooms, control was maintained through respect and the fact that all of these teachers were familiar with each individual student they taught. Though they challenged him academically, the quality Vernon remembered most about these teachers concerned the affective side of the educational experience. More than twenty years later, he still holds a warm place in his heart for these men and recalls the feelings of self-worth that were created from the time he spent in their classrooms. Another thing that impressed Vernon about these favorite teachers was that each of them extended themselves to all students, regardless of race, ethnicity, gender, socio-economic levels, or social standing within the school.

Aubrey's story of teachers was framed by her children's experiences and the classrooms that were selected for them. Her favorite teacher was a woman who taught Jackson and Elizabeth in third grade. This teacher required all parents to be part of the classroom in meaningful ways by volunteering at least once per month. Communication with parents was open and democratic, demonstrated by this teacher's desire to listen to other classroom members. Aubrey described the fine balance this teacher was able to maintain between leading and listening. This teacher also challenged her students academically and constructed a positive classroom community.

Sorry to say, this was an isolated experience of teaching excellence in the children's public school experience. Aubrey and her children were disappointed with many of the other teachers in the public schools. Reviewing the structure of the public school system and the environment in which teachers were required to work prompted Aubrey to characterize the job of teaching as almost impossible. First and foremost, she recognized the importance of the role of teacher and the incredible responsibility that came with the job of preparing America's children for the future. She also felt that teachers in the state were underpaid and overworked, resulting in low self-esteem, poor motivation, and the lack of a desire to work in their students' best interest. Most of all, Aubrey felt the teachers were unhappy in their jobs and that the joy of teaching was just not there. Much of what was wrong with the public schools was not the fault of the teachers or the structure of the public school institution itself, but rather the population of students who entered school that were unprepared for learning.

The children in the study provided wonderful insights into the practice of teaching in both public school and home school environments. Hearing the voice of the child certainly brought a sense of authenticity to this emergent theme on teachers. Elizabeth characterized good teachers as people who "do not scream a lot." Apparently, Elizabeth had experienced many teachers who used this technique to manage their classrooms. The third grade teacher of whom Aubrey spoke was also Elizabeth's favorite teacher. This teacher provided her students with the flexibility to move around the classroom and interact with learning centers staffed with parent volunteers. Elizabeth felt that she learned a lot in third grade and appreciated the way her teacher gave respect to the students and challenged them to do their best. This teacher also rewarded students for proper behavior and effort in completing classroom assignments and homework.

Elizabeth also mentioned trust as an important component in her definition of the perfect teacher. This was a quality she identified in her mother during her home schooling practice. Elizabeth commented that she could always trust her mother in making the best decisions for her regardless of the fact that she did not always agree with Aubrey's decisions and actions.

Jackson's reflections on teachers focused on the art of

teaching and the sense of fairness that was created by them. The majority of his teachers would not go into enough depth when covering classroom subjects. Jackson recalled that his teachers would skim over the main ideas but never really expose the true depth of a subject. Jackson found this practice frustrating and commented that few teachers would respond to his follow up questions in his true desire to learn more about a subject. With the help of his mother after school, Jackson would research areas of study from the classroom.

The teachers Jackson favored possessed a quality of fairness and justice in running their classrooms. These teachers managed their classes with a sense of respect and treated all students the same. Jackson, like Elizabeth, identified these qualities in his mother and felt fortunate to have experienced those qualities in home schooling.

Critique of Public Schools

All participants had much to offer in regard to their experiences with public schools. To Aubrey, many of the issues regarding public schools stemmed from her view of the public school as gatekeeper and overseer of knowledge. In her opinion, what was most important to the institution was following its own agenda. This agenda positioned parents and children as subservient to the school, rather than in a partnered relationship of combined effort to educate. She gave several examples through personal experiences and the experiences of others of the institution serving its own needs. In each case, school administrators were unwilling to consider alternative measures to meet individual student needs.

In her critique of public schools, Aubrey made it clear that she believed schools valued education but that few students came to school with a desire to learn. Consequently, the priority of schools today has more to do with behavior management than with true learning and teaching. Aubrey resented the time her children spent waiting for other kids to "settle down." In addition, she felt that teachers were unprepared to deal with the frequent behavior problems that occurred in school.

Violence in public schools was another area of concern for Aubrey. Every day in the media, she learned about threats, assaults, and killings that would go on in the schools. Living in a society that values handguns undoubtedly filters down into our schools at all levels, including elementary. Aubrey had no questions about structuring her children's lives to avoid contact with others who presented the possibility of harm and serious risk. Home schooling provided Aubrey with the control she needed in this restructuring.

The final area of concern that Aubrey voiced was centered on the classroom curriculum. Having spent many hours in the classroom as a volunteer, she recognized the very basic level of what was being taught. This realization was very disappointing to Aubrey and proved to be the major reason for her move toward home schooling. Aubrey continues to search for that special school that provides a challenging course of study, includes the elements of care and safety, and encourages a learning partnership between all stakeholders.

Vernon provided many insightful comments. His discussion began by characterizing his own K-12 public school experience as "wonderful," where caring teachers and challenging curricula were combined with small class sizes. The majority of his teachers really knew him as a person and made it known that he just wasn't another kid in class. If Vernon could have his way of improving public schools, he would reduce the student class size, hire more teachers, and improve school facilities.

Vernon went on to characterize the curriculum as "watered down" to the point where its meaning and relevancy to the students' lives were lost. To him, low expectations equaled low performance. Vernon admitted that the changes he suggested would more than double the capital expenditure for public education, but that these improvements would facilitate the development of students who possessed a positive self image, a sense of belonging, and civic competence.

Being the problem solver that he is, Vernon recommended that one way to improve schools would be to bring a sense of family and home into the public school. The feeling of family would make kids feel connected to the learning community. He felt the sense of home could be facilitated by embracing the idea that all stakeholders were valued and were regarded as an integral part of the school community. In his experiences with his own children in public school, Vernon perceived the schools and parents in a divorced relationship where each party blamed or passed responsibility of action or inaction on to the other. Key to this partnership was the revival of the concept of responsibility where stakeholders would deal with consequences. Vernon felt students, and parents too at times, were not accustomed to dealing with the natural consequences of their actions. Constructing clear expectations for student behavior and following up with fair and equitable consequences would definitely provide a secure and comfortable atmosphere for all stakeholders.

The third element of bringing home into school included

a focus on parenting before the child ever enters the public school grounds. Vernon commented that parenting is paramount to everything that goes on in school and should reinforce the idea of respect for others in the world as well as help guide children to an understanding of boundaries of appropriate behavior. Vernon recognizes a plethora of absent parents who neither teach limits of acceptable behavior nor desire to be involved with their children in meaningful ways. In response to this social condition, Vernon asked if it would be unreasonable for public schools to offer classes in parenting and human relations. These course offerings would have the dual purpose of making the school curriculum relevant to life as well as offering valuable information by providing a perspective on the maintenance of human relationships. I couldn't agree more with him.

Elizabeth's experience with public school began in a flourish of academic and social success. Even when she was sick, Elizabeth hated to miss one moment of school. Teachers played a large part in her view of school. She especially liked her third grade teacher who provided her with the freedom to move at her own pace and who presented the curriculum in interesting ways. This teacher was, unfortunately, the exception to the rule. Most of her other teachers lacked the quality of respect when interacting with her and the other students and did not treat everyone in a fair way. Elizabeth began to get tired of the student/teacher relationship based on authority and, as a result, looked toward home schooling as a solution.

Elizabeth's critique of the public schools was naturally focused on the people who represented the institution: namely, the teachers. From her perspective as a child,

Elizabeth was able to recognize the power dynamics that occurred within the institution through the actions of the teacher. The perceptions that Elizabeth mentioned included the fact that teachers really didn't like involved parents nor did they want to share their power with classroom "outsiders." Many of the same techniques her former teachers used in quieting students were used on the parents. These teacher behaviors included over-talking, raising the voice, not listening, interrupting, and becoming "preachy" by dictating a whole litany of ethical and moral right and wrong behaviors. The teachers' unwillingness to exchange ideas and create authentic dialogue was symptomatic of the conditions of the school institution itself mentioned by Vernon and Aubrey in their discussion of power, agenda, and partnership. I viewed Elizabeth as very astute in her perceptions of the relationships in which she was involved.

Jackson also viewed the school institution through the actions of his teachers. The simplified curriculum of which he spoke earlier was probably a reflection of the school district's standards rather than the teacher's ability to deliver a rich educational experience. In school, Jackson was troubled by the wait time he would have to endure and the often unfair classroom practices that he perceived. Jackson recalled inadequacies and injustices in the classroom setting. Thinking that "teachers were teachers," he felt he should just do what he was told. Though Jackson really didn't like what was going on, he had a live and let live attitude toward the time he spent in public school.

Jackson also expressed concern that the majority of the teachers' time was spent on the kids who had behavior problems. Jackson estimated that he spent less than two hours a day in learning activities under the direction of his teachers. In this same area, he also commented that there were some nice kids in school, but there were also some kids with whom he had to be very careful. Some of these kids were prone to misbehavior and bullying. These kids sometimes played a significant part in the instructional process and shaped the school experience in negative ways. Jackson recognized the positive and negative aspects of social interaction in school and commented that the positive social component in school was very important to learning and one that he enjoyed. The lack of peer interaction was what he disliked most about the education program at home.

The Aporia of Public School Education

All participants expressed concern with what was not present in the public schools and the mixed messages that they often received from principals and teachers. To Aubrey, what was missing from the public school experience was the desire on the part of school personnel to enter into a partnership with parents and students based on mutuality. This lack of relationship in the process of learning was identified through her discussion of the school's agenda in chapter one. Aubrey commented that the school's agenda was paramount to all other stakeholder concerns. This missing element of consideration for the needs of students and families translated further into her recognition of the absence of care in schools. Aubrey was also concerned about the lack of safety in schools. This aporia is one of the most serious issues in regard to public school education. Aubrey did not feel certain that her children would be free from harm in the public school environment.

This attitude was reinforced by numerous stories from friends and public school students and the many instances of violence reported by the local and national media.

To Vernon, aporia was played out through the absence of personal connections his children made with their teachers. Vernon commented that with large class sizes and the overwhelming responsibilities teachers have in performing their duties, they seldom have time for relationship building. Vernon remembered three teachers in particular during his high school years who focused on the affective side of education and who made it their responsibility to know every student and make them feel important. Here, the missing element in public schools is the lack of relationship between students and teachers.

Aporia in the sense of contradiction arose when Vernon spoke about consequences for inappropriate student behaviors. Though schools do make provisions for the expectations of student behaviors, consequences for misbehavior are often not enforced. Vernon felt that kids needed boundaries for their behavior and that schools should find fair ways of enacting consequences that reinforce acceptable behavior.

Both parents in this study mentioned the absence of a learning environment that encouraged excellence in education. To Aubrey, public schools were more interested in providing for the needs of children with behavior problems than with kids who were serious about learning. Vernon concurred that the absence of high expectations for student learning certainly did not serve the best interest of his children.

Jackson also recognized the lack of challenge the public school classroom offered him. He commented that his attempts to gain a deeper understanding of the material in class were not encouraged by teachers. Jackson often felt ignored by teachers who would not answer his questions and who sometimes made him feel silly for asking them. Another aporia that Jackson mentioned concerned student voice and the lack of input he had into his studies. Jackson commented, "Teachers are teachers." He went on to explain that he learned to follow directions and do what the teacher told him regardless of whether it made sense to him or not. This lack of dialogue with his teachers led Jackson to question the degree to which his teachers cared about him and the other students. Jackson was very aware of issues concerning care and fairness and commented that he rarely experienced feelings of care from his teachers in public school. In late January, Jackson left the public charter school he had been attending since August to return to home schooling. On the day of his withdrawal, the principal and several teachers came up to Jackson and told him that they would miss him and that they were sorry he was leaving. Jackson was perplexed and didn't know what to think. Jackson told me that he had no idea that anyone even knew him, let alone missed him. For Jackson, the aporia of public school education was the attention to the ethic of care and the subsequent relationships that developed as the result.

To Elizabeth, public schools did not provide challenging academic programs. Much of her time was spent waiting for other students to be quiet or for them to catch up with the teacher. Also absent was the opportunity for deep study and understanding into her area of interest. For Elizabeth, this was math. In the perfect world, she would like her educational program to center around math where she could really accelerate her learning and become an expert in the area. This was almost impossible in the public school setting. In this case, the aporia was flexibility in designing curriculum to focus on student strengths and interests.

The Beauty of Home Schooling

Aubrey described the sense of freedom and independence she felt in her role as home schooling teacher. In home schooling, each child's educational program was tailored to meet his or her needs and interests. In home schooling, the world of learning opened up to her and she realized that learning was everywhere and in everything. Also, the children played a large role in developing the subjects they studied. This component allowed the kids to buy into the learning activities, take ownership of them, and truly enjoy the whole process of learning. To Aubrey, home schooling provided a much better experience in connecting learning to life than in the public schools. Home schooling opened Aubrey's eyes in an epiphanic way that led her to the realization that there was a whole other side to education that had nothing to do with school. In fact, she commented that the most important things she had learned in life were far removed from the school/classroom environment. Learning through living and contact with the real world of experiences was the driving force behind home schooling.

Most importantly, the beauty of her home schooling experience was in the strong family relationships that were created through close personal interactions. When the children began their home schooling journey together, both Aubrey and Vernon recognized the children's return of their love for learning and a renewal of the affection their children once had for them. As Aubrey commented, "They were no longer afraid to love me." If this were the sole gift given through the home schooling experience, to Aubrey, it would have been enough.

It took Vernon about one year before he bought into the idea of home schooling for his family. The component of his children's studies at home that convinced him the most of home schooling's benefits was when Aubrey and the kids were able to just get up and go and use their field trip experiences as a stimulus for learning. Like Aubrey, Vernon began to see that learning was everywhere and in everything. As Vernon witnessed the children's transition from "artificial" learning to learning in the world, he became interested in the natural flow of the mind and the way children can make connections to seemingly unrelated ideas. He also recognized that this bending and shaping by the natural learner was often not tolerated in the traditional public school setting where instruction progressed in a typically linear fashion. Home schooling sang to the natural flow and the possibilities for authentic learning that was imbedded in it.

The beauty of home schooling was also that it capitalized on the teachable moments that presented themselves unannounced from time to time. Vernon's embrace of home schooling came with his realization of the ubiquitous nature of learning and the tremendous academic gains the children displayed. For Vernon, the beauty of home schooling was in the way it facilitated and strengthened the family bonds, which was so important.

Elizabeth commented that she loved home schooling because she could work up to her true potential and not have to wait for other kids. Elizabeth's identity was shaped in part by her strong academic abilities. Home schooling helped to encourage and promote this academic excellence by letting her move at her own pace and, at the same time, allowing her to study the areas of her true interests. Home schooling also allowed her to spend time with her mom whom she loves and trusts. Elizabeth commented that having the time to spend with her mother was one of the most wonderful things about home schooling.

Home schooling allowed Elizabeth to take some interesting field trips. Elizabeth loved getting out and learning about all the things in life, ranging from the workings of the Very Large Array Telescopes in Socorro to seeing how violins were made in a local music shop. These trips served as the impetus for Elizabeth's discovery style of learning, which kept her continually engaged.

In home schooling, Elizabeth was also able to take classes in the community during the day on a variety of subjects where she met other kids and developed new friendships. Elizabeth developed her social contacts through this avenue and felt satisfied in connecting with her peers in this way. To Elizabeth, the beauty of home schooling was in the ability to progress at her own pace, to study what interested her, and in spending time with her mother. Elizabeth continues to home school and looks forward to home schooling in the future.

Jackson was the first family member to advocate for home schooling. What impressed him the most were the fun projects and field trips that his mother had planned. The first project in which Jackson was involved was the writing of a family newspaper. Through this medium, Jackson communicated with extended family members and learned much about his own background. Jackson enjoyed working on this project that was centered around his life and the lives of his family.

Like Elizabeth, Jackson also found pleasure in the field

trips that he and his family took. Jackson characterized many of these trips as "fascinating." The beauty of home schooling was being able to interact with the environment around him and experience life directly, not reading about it from behind a desk. Jackson also enjoyed the times he spent around the house during the day. He told one story about a time he walked the dogs around the block after attaching them to his scooter, with which he reached breakneck speeds. Jackson found beauty in simple events like this and others that he experienced during his time in home school. To Jackson and all the other members of his family, having the time to connect with one another through the learning experiences of his choice revealed the beauty behind his home schooling practice.

Chapter Six:

Discovering the Boundaries of Home Schooling in America

Home schooling is one of the least studied, but one of the fastest growing phenomena in American public education (Archer 2000). The National Home Education Research Institute reports that in the year 2000, 1.5 to 1.9 million school-aged children were home schooled in the United States (2% of the total student population), and that the phenomenon of home schooling, according to the United States Department of Education, has a growth rate of 15% per year (Archer 2000). The National Center for Education Statistics in its July 2001 report gives a more conservative estimate of the number of home schooling children (US Department of Education 2001). The estimate at the 95% confidence interval for the number of home schooled students, ages 5 through 17, with a grade equivalent of kindergarten to grade twelve is in the range of 709,00 to 992,000 individuals with a mean count of 850,000 individuals being home schooled during spring 1999 (US Department of Education 1999). Though discrepancies do exist between the National Home Education Research Institute and the United States Department of Education estimates of the number of home schooling children, these figures do represent a significant number of children and families who are serving their educational needs through the alternative means of home schooling.

At present, policymakers and school officials make countless decisions and form school district regulations about this relatively unexplored area of education without accurate information or a theoretical or philosophical background to support sound decision-making practices. In addition, policymakers at the school district level do not have the benefit and support of teacher organizations such as the National Education Association in establishing much needed dialogue regarding cooperative policies and practices with home schooling communities. The NEA characterizes home schooling education as poor. The NEA also proposes that all home schoolers be required to take exams at specified intervals during the school year and that formal instruction be delivered by certified personnel in order to ensure success for the home schooled student.

To many home schooling families, the formal delivery of educational services through use of textbooks, worksheets, and tests does not constitute successful teaching practice. Success to many home schooling families is defined in broader terms than scores and grades on tests and other traditional measures of performance. True educational experiences are played out by the learner's authentic integration of meaningful information and its application in authentic life situations. To home schooling families who identify themselves as the "unschooled," education is considered to be a natural process that embraces the curiosity of the child and his/her innate desire for learning. Home schooling families who do utilize curriculum-based instruction often do so through extension activities such as field trips, internships, family vacations, experiments, libraries, and information gathering through the Internet.

In coming to terms with these politically charged points of view in regard to the legitimacy of home schooling, the realization that a better understanding of the home schooling movement and a more informed concept of the nature of this phenomenon is needed.

This important and growing area deserves study for several reasons. First of all, with a better understanding of the home schooled population, educators may find themselves in a better position to provide a more responsive and meaningful educational experience for all children. If we challenged ourselves to understand the educational dynamics that occur in the home school setting, we may be able to discover and transfer valuable methods, materials, and insights used at home to improve educational practices in public schools.

In a *Time* magazine article (August 27, 2001, "Home Sweet Home"), John McCloud and Jodie Morse report that, "The average home schooler's SAT score is 1000, 80 points higher than the average score for the general population." Addressing issues of home schooling in the context of aporia in public school education also forces us to review teaching practices and roles.

In the US Department of Education's 1999 report on home schooling, parents were asked to list their reasons for home schooling. First on the list was, "Can give child a better education at home." Listening to and understanding the home school community's difficulties with public education may provide us with the insight needed for curriculum revision, change, and the eventual evolution to improve the services and programs provided.

Secondly, a deeper understanding of the home schoolers' critique of public education may also provide insight into the role of the teacher. According to Grozier (1999), in his article, "It's a case of we know when we're not wanted: The parent's perspective on parent-teacher roles and responsibilities," teachers continue to reinforce the idea of parents as passive members in the process of learning and teachers who serve as the professionals who know best. This parent disenfranchisement from the process of educating children is another major reason why families choose home schooling as an alternative to public education.

One of the most basic reasons for why I call for additional research in the subject of home schooling is the fact that school district bureaucrats who regulate and control home schooling practices must have accurate and relevant information in order to make informed decisions. With base line information, as well as insights into the nature of the social structure of home schooling families, policies on home schooling can be relevant, helpful, and equitable.

Finally, study into the area of home schooling would facilitate the needed dialogue between public school and home school partners. This dialogue would certainly produce a wealth of shared knowledge into methods of teaching, as well as insights into the critical teacher/student/parent relationship. If we allow ourselves to be mindful of the intentions and actions of home schooling families, we may be able to construct a more meaningful public education program. By utilizing home school practices and philosophies in concert with an authentic self-critique, we may discover profound implications for how public education institutions conduct the business of teaching and learning towards excellence for *all* America's children.

Selected Bibliography

Abbott, J., & T. Ryan. 1999. Constructing knowledge, reconstructing schools. *Educational Leadership* 57 (3):66–69.

Agger, B. 1992. *Cultural studies as critical theory.* Philadelphia: The Falmer Press.

Anderson, G. L., K. Herr, & A.S. Nihlen. 1994. *Studying your own school: An educator's guide to qualitative practitioner research.* Thousand Oaks, CA: Corwin Press, Inc.

Apple, M. W. 2000. The cultural politics of homeschooling. *Peabody Journal of Education* 75 (1):156–71.

Arai, B. 1999. Homeschooling and the redefinition of citizenship. Education Policy Analysis Archives. Available from htpp://epaa.asu.edu/

Archer, J. 1999. Unexplored territory. *Education Week* 19 (15):25–28.

Archer, J. 2000. Home study. *Teacher Magazine* 11 (5):18–20.

Barz, J. M. 2000. Turning our hearts towards home (schoolers). *Lutheran Education* 35 (3):122–23.

Blair, J. 2000. New colleges set to welcome home-schooled students in the fall: Patrick Henry College in Virginia. *Education Week* 19 (29):5.

Bracy, G. W. 1999. A tale of two studies. *Phi Delta Kappan* 98 (10):789–99.

Carper, J. 2000. Pluralism to establish dissent: The religious and educational context of homeschooling. *Peabody Journal of Education* 75 (1):8–19.

Caruana, V. 1999. Partnering with homeschoolers: Part time education in the public schools. *Educational Leadership* 57 (1):58–60.

Chen, E. J. 1999. Computer use in homeschool families. *DAI* 60 (01A):58–60.

Clinton, W. 1997. *One America: The President's initiative on race.* Available from htpp://www.whitehouse.gov/Initiatives/OneAmerica/events.html#oaotm

Cloud, J. "Outside, wanting in." *Time,* 27 December 1999.

Cloud, J., & J. Morse. "Home sweet home." *Time,* 27 August 2001.

Colfax, D., & M. Colfax. 1988. *Homeschooling for excellence.* New York, NY: Warner Books.

Coulter, A. 2000. Homeschooling gets inadvertent boost from the United States Supreme Court. *Human Events* 56 (25):1.

Denzin, N. K. 1989. *Interpretive interactionism.* Newbury Park, CA: Sage Publications Inc.

Denzin, N. K. 1997. *Interpretive ethnography: Ethnographic practices for the 21st century.* Thousand Oaks, CA: Sage Publications Inc.

Denzin, N. K., & Y. S. Lincoln. 1994. *Handbook of qualitative research.* Thousand Oaks, CA: Sage Publications, Inc.

Dewey, J. 1938. *Experience and education.* New York, NY: Kappa Delta Pi.

Donegan, K. 1998. Self esteem. AERA-G Division G: *Social Context of Education Online.* Available from aerag@asuvm.iinre.asu.edu/.

Duffey, C. 2000. *Christian educators' curriculum manual: Elementary grades.* United States: Grove Publishers.

Duffey, J. 1999. Homeschooling and students in special education: Sorting out the options for parents. *Preventing School Failure* 43 (2):57–53.

Duvall, S., & D. Ward. 1997. An exploratory study of home-school instructional environments. *Education and Treatment of Children* 20 (2):20–35.

Edison, C. 1982. *Schooling for work and working at school: Perspectives on immigrant and working-class education in urban America, 1880–1920.* Cambridge, MA: Ballinger Publishing Company.

Ensign, J. 2000. Defying the stereotypes of special education: Homeschool students. *Peabody Journal of Education* 75 (1):147–58.

Erlanson, D. A., E. L. Harris, B. L. Skipper, & S. D. Allen. 1993. *Doing naturalistic inquiry: A guide to methods.* Newbury Park, CA: Sage Publications, Inc.

Farris, M. P., & S. Woodruff. 2000. The future of homeschooling, *Peabody Journal of Education* 75 (1):233–55.

Foucault, M. 1981. *The history of sexuality (Vol. 1).* Harmondsworth, UK: Pelican Publishing.

Garza, M. 1999. Home invasion ruling. *Reason* 30 (10):12.

Glaser, B., & A. Strauss. 1968. *The discovery of grounded theory.* London: Weidenfield and Nicolson Publishing.

Greenfield, N. Boomtime for homeschoolers. *The Times Educational Supplement,* 21 April 2000.

Griffin, M. 1999. *The homeschooling handbook: From preschool to high school, a parent's guide. (Rev 2nd ed.).* US: The H. W. Wilson Company.

Grove, P. B. 1986. *Webster's third new international dictionary of the English language unabridged.* Springfield, MA: Merriam Webster Inc.

Grozier, G. 1999. Is it a case of, "We know when we're not wanted?" The parents' perspective on parent-teacher roles and relationships. *Educational Research* 41 (3):315–28.

Grubb, D. 1998. Homeschooling: Who and why? Paper presented at the 27th annual meeting of the Mid-South Educational Research Association 3–6 November, New Orleans, LA.

Guterson, D. 1992. *Family Matters: Why Homeschooling Makes Sense.* New York: Harcourt, Brace and Company.

Hawkins, D. 1996. Culture and ideas: Homeschool battles. *U.S. News and World Report Online.* Available from http://www.usnews.com/usnews/issue/school.htm/

Hill, P. T. 2000. Homeschooling and the future of public education. *Peabody Journal of Education* 75 (1):20–31.

Holt, J. 1964. *How children fail.* New York: Pitman Publishing Corporation.

Holt, J. 1969. *The underachieving school.* New York: Dell Publishing Company.

Hooks, B. 1984. *Feminist theory: From margin to center.* Boston: South End Press.

Jenkins, M. 1994. Homeschooling: Government policy. Alberta *ReportNews Magazine* 21 (29):33.

John, W. 2000. The ultimate (un)school choice. *Christian Science Monitor* 92 (222):20.

Johnston, M. 1997. *Contradictions on collaboration: New thinking on school/university partnerships.* New York: Teacher's College Press.

Kelly, K. "Homeschooling." *U.S. News and World Report,* 13 November 2000.

Kirsch, G. E. 1999. *Ethical dilemmas in feminist research: The politics of location, interpretation, and publication.* Albany: State University of New York Press.

Klugewicz, S. L., & C. Carraccio. 1999. Homeschooled children: A pediatric perspective. *Clinical Pediatrics* 38 (7):47.

Kohn, A. 1998. Only for my kid: How privileged parents undermine school reform. *Phi Delta Kappan* 79:568–578.

Labaree, D. 1997. Public goods, private goods: The American struggle over educational goals. *American Educational Research Journal* 34 (1):39–81.

Lasch, C. 1995. *The revolt of the elites and the betrayal of democracy*. New York: Norton Publishing.

Lather, P. 1991. *Getting smart: Feminist research and pedagogy within the post modern.* New York: Routledge.

Learner, S. Maverick: Bill Wetzel. *The Utne Reader,* March 2000.

Lincoln, Y. S., & E. G. Guba. 1985. *Naturalistic inquiry.* Beverly Hills, CA: Sage Publications Inc.

Lines, P. A. 2000. When homeschoolers go to school: A partnership. *Peabody Journal of Education* 75 (1):159–86.

Lubinski, C. 2000. Whither the common good? A critique of homeschooling. *Peabody Journal of Education* 75 (1):207–32.

Mason, R. 1999. *Homeschooling all the way through high school.* United States: Tyndale House Publishers.

Mayberry, M. 1991. Conflict and social determinism: The reprivatization of education. Paper presented at the American Educational Research Association meeting, 3–7 April, Chicago.

McDowell, S. A. 2000. The homeschooling mother-teacher: Toward a theory of social integration. *Peabody Journal of Education* 75 (1):187–206.

McDowell, S. A., A. Sanchez, & S. Jones. 2000. Participation and perception: Looking at homeschooling through a multicultural lens. *Peabody Journal of Education* 75 (1):124–46.

Medlin, R. G. 2000. Homeschooling and the question of socialization. *Peabody Journal of Education* 75 (1):107–23.

Meighan, R. 1995. Home-based education effectiveness research and some of its implications. *Educational Review* 47 (3):275–85.

Menendez, A. 1996. *Homeschooling: The facts.* Silver Spring, MD: Americans for Religious Liberty.

Merriam, S. B. 1998. *Qualitative research and case study applications in education.* San Francisco, CA: Josey-Bass Publishers.

Miles, M., & A. Huberman. 1994. *Qualitative data analysis: An expanded source book.* Thousand Oaks, CA: Sage Publishing.

Mintz, S., & S. Kellogg. 1990. The Americans domestic revolutions: A social history of American family life. *History* 75 (245):449.

Montgomery, L. 1989. The effect of homeschooling on the leadership skills of homeschooled students. *Homeschool Researcher* 5 (1):1–10.

Morgan, M. L., J. Allee, M. Mindeman, & J. Guest. 1999. *Homeschooling on a shoestring; A jam packed guide.* New York: State University of New York Press.

Myers, D. T. 1997. *Feminist social thought: A reader.* New York: Routledge.

Narigon, C. 2001. The end and beginning of homeschooling. *Home Education Magazine* 18 (5):10–12.

Nodding, N. 1992. *The challenge to care in schools: An alternative approach to education.* New York: Teachers College Press.

Parker, B. 1999. Parent-child relationship, home learning environment, and school readiness. *School Psychology Review* 2 (3):413.

Paulson, A. 2000. Where the school is home. *Christian Science Monitor* 92 (222):18.

Pipho, C. 2000. Choice options on the increase. *Phi Delta Kappan* 81 (8):565–66.

Ray, B. D. 2000. Homeschooling for individuals' gain and society's common good. *Peabody Journal of Education* 75 (1):272–93.

Ricke, K., 1999. *Public school superintendents' perceptions of cooperative sponsorships with homeschools for extracurricular activities in Minnesota.* Master's thesis, St. Cloud University, St. Cloud, MN.

Riley, R. W. 1999. Home is where the heart is. *Education* 120 (1):6–7.

Rudner, L. 1999. Scholastic achievement and demographics characteristics of homeschool children in 1998. *Education Policy Analysis Archives* 7 (8). Available from http://epaa.asuedu/epaa/v7n8.

Rutkowski, K. M. 1998. Homeschool pioneers on the web. *Multimedia Schools* 5 (3):76–80.

Sandel, M. 1996. *Democracy's discontent: America in search of public policy.* Cambridge, MA: Harvard University Press.

Schmechebier, C. 1927. *The office of Indian affairs.* Baltimore, MD: Johns Hopkins University Press.

Seidman, I. E. 1991. *Interviewing as qualitative research.* New York: Teachers College Press.

Sergiovanni, T. J. 1992. *Moral leadership: Getting to the heart of school improvement.* San Francisco: Jossey-Bass Publishers, Inc.

Scheps, S. G. 1999. Homeschoolers in the library. *School Library Journal* 45 (2):38.

Sowell, T. 1996. Education or power play? *Headway* 8 (9):20.

Spradley, J. P., & D. W. McCurdy. 1972. *The cultural experience.* Chicago: Science Research Associates, Inc.

Spring, J. 1982. *The evolving political structure of American schooling.* Cambridge, MA: Ballinger Publishing Company.

Staehle, D. 2000. Taking a different path: A mother's reflections on homeschooling. *Roper Review* 22 (4):270–71.

Starratt, R. J. 1997. *Building an ethical school: A practical response to the moral crisis in schools.* Washington, DC: The Falmer Press.

Stringer, E. T. 1996. *Action research.* Thousand Oaks, CA: Sage Publications, Inc.

Stringer, E. T. 1999. *Action research: (2nd ed.).* Thousand Oaks, CA: Sage Publications Inc.

Taylor, L. A. 1997. Home on school: Insights on education through the lens of homeschoolers. *Theory into practice* 36 (2):110.

Tyack, D. B. 1974. *The one best system: A history of urban American education.* Cambridge, MA: Harvard University Press.

Tyler, Z. P., & J. Carper. 2000. From confrontation to accommodation: Homeschooling in South Carolina. *Peabody Journal of Education* 75 (1):32–48.

Vygotsky, L. S. 1962. *Thought and language.* Cambridge, MA: MIT Press.

United States Office of Accounting. 1997. In a report to the Honorable Byron L. Dorgan, U.S. Senate on 1 December 1997, GAO/HEHS, 47–98.

United States Department of Education. 1999. *Homeschooling in the United States.* Parent Survey of the National Household Education Surveys Program (NHES:1999). Available from htpp://www.nces.ed.gov/pubs2001/2001033.pdf/

United States Department of Education. 2000. *Digest of Education Statistics* (ED 1.326.2000). Washington, DC: U.S. Government Printing Office.

Weedon, C. 1998. *Feminist practice and postructuralist theory: (2nd ed.).* Malden, MA: Blackwell Publishers Inc.

Welner, K., & K. Welner. 1999. Contextualizing homeschooling data: A response to Rudner. *Education Policy Analysis Archives* 7 (8). Available from http://epaa.asu.edu/epaa/v7no13.html.

Whitman, W. 1968. *Leaves of grass.* New York: New York Public Library.

Wilson, G.B. 1997. It does take a village. *America* 176 (14):10.

About the Author

Dr. Higgins had been an advocate of home schooling long before he and his wife entered into home schooling practice with their daughter.

With more than twenty years working in public education in domestic and overseas locations, Higgins' interests and efforts in education have focused on the integration of the ethic of care into the classroom curriculum, and the development of differentiated learning strategies and opportunities for students in grades K-12.

Though his permanent home is in New Mexico, Dr. Higgins also spends time on the island of Hawaii where he works with an intensive program for special needs students.